"*Simply A Whisper* leaves you craving God's whispers into your own life. Enlightening and encouraging. This book will take you on a journey into God's genuine love for you."

—BARBARA MEISS,
Vice President of "Meiss Education Institute"

"I truly appreciate the life and ministry of Lenni Nordloh. This dear servant has a deep passion to know and walk with God. In her book, **Simply a Whisper,** Lenni traces the biblical truth that God speaks to His people in real and personal ways. In a day when many believers give such little time to prayer, this book is an encouragement to slow down and listen. May God help His people to hunger for His smallest whisper."

—DR. GREGORY FRIZZELL,
Prayer and Spiritual Awakening Specialist
Baptist General Convention of Oklahoma
Oklahoma City, Oklahoma

"Lenni has a way with words that says it all. If you 'want' to hear Him **Whisper** and 'want' to learn ways to hear Him, this is a must read book. She has shown me how to listen"

—MARY JACOBSON,
A New Believer and Member of Superstition
Buttes Christian Fellowship (Retired long haul truck driver)
Apache Junction, Arizona

Simply a Whisper

Learn to Listen for the Still Small Voice of God

Lenni Nordloh

WestBow°
PRESS
A DIVISION OF THOMAS NELSON
& ZONDERVAN

National Huguenot Society website, http://www.huguenot.netnation.com

WestBow Press books may be ordered through booksellers or by contacting:

WestBow Press
A Division of Thomas Nelson & Zondervan
1663 Liberty Drive
Bloomington, IN 47403
www.westbowpress.com
1 (866) 928-1240

ISBN: 978-1-4908-5248-5 (sc)
ISBN: 978-1-4908-5247-8 (e)

Library of Congress Control Number: 2014916655

Printed in the United States of America.

WestBow Press rev. date: 10/13/2014

CONTENTS

DEDICATION

I want to dedicate this book to the memory of my mother-in-law, Margaret Roselyn Nordloh, who passed away on November 1, 2011. She was one of my biggest fans and encouraged me to continue to write because she said that I wrote simple enough for the ordinary person to understand the truth of God's love.

FORWARD

"Your eyes saw my unformed body; all the days ordained for me were written in your book before one of them came to be."
Psalm 139:16 NIV

L enora (Lenni) Nordloh, before she was born, God knew who she would grow up to be. He made her to teach and inspire many generations of His children. When He sent her into this world, He sent her knowing she would be a champion for His throne.

I had the privilege of meeting Lenni and her husband, Marty somewhere between winning champions for Christ, while battling cancer, and winning champions for Christ, while surviving cancer. There is nothing on this earth that could slow these two down on their mission for our Lord. The message He is sending us today through Lenni is this: My voice is simply a whisper.

While God has an everlasting strength and a roaring voice at times (Job 37:2), some of the most important messages we will ever hear are those that come in a still, small whisper:

> *"…a great and powerful wind tore the mountains apart and shattered the rocks before the Lord, but the Lord was not in the wind. After the wind there was an earthquake, but the Lord was not in the earthquake. After the earthquake came a fire, but the Lord was not in the fire. And after the fire, came a gentle whisper."*

That moment poor Elijah knew he was in trouble! It is like the point in your life when you know you really did something awful and all your mother or father says to you in that quiet way is, "I am so disappointed."

Thankfully in this book, Lenni teaches us that God can tell us many things while whispering to us. She also teaches how we can listen for this whisper, which I have found is the most important aspect when trying to understand what actions God wants us to take. I firmly believe learning the lessons taught through Lenni in this book will significantly enhance your personal time with God. I cannot wait to hear the reviews from those who take the time to read this book and move their lives closer to God.

Enjoy!

Jacquelyn Hornady

PREFACE

The last 40 years my husband and I have been in the ministry. Sometime during those 40 years we first became church volunteers and then my husband said that he wanted to go to seminary at the Golden Gate Baptist Theological Seminary in Mill Valley, California. We both attended, but my husband went on to get his Divinity Degree. Our first mission opportunity was located near Cheyenne, Wyoming where we served for 5 years.

The next church where we served in was in Florence, Arizona when we became acquainted with and studied "Experiencing God" by Henry Blackaby and Claude King. This study turned our life around when the study said "God is always at work around you" and "God could ask you do something you cannot do". Over the next 20 years we have facilitated over 20 plus classes, along with reading and teaching the Bible. We have observed God's Holy Spirit at work in and around people's lives. We have seen the activity of God for ourselves, so while in prayer, the Holy Spirit whispered His desire for me to write "Simply a Whisper".

The writing of "Simply a Whisper" was written within 6 months, but sharing the chapters with other professionals, they recommended that continued prayer would open new chapters that would touch people's hearts. The book sat for two years on my computer, when the diagnosis of breast cancer took me in a different direction. The journey made me get closer to what the Lord wanted to say through me to encourage others in their walk with the Lord. My prayer was "Bless me, Lord, so that my life will glorify you!" Then the book was revisited and 10 new chapters were written over the next year.

Open your heart and listen for God's messages that He wants to give you. I can truthfully say that is can be "Simply a Whisper".

May the Lord Bless you,

Lenni Nordloh

INTRODUCTION

Does God speak to people today? Could it be that He speaks to His people in a gentle Whisper? The book was written to encourage you to become spiritually sensitive to God's whispers. The first chapters are simple ways that you may hear, but later it starts to reveal deeper thoughts that will touch your heart.

When you read the Old Testament of the Bible through, you may notice that God seems to speak to various personalities in different ways. Adam was told by God to name all the animals. Then He created the woman so that man would not be alone. He gave instructions that they both could eat of any tree accept the fruit in the middle of the garden. He told them to be fruitful and multiply. There are several documented conversations between God and Adam. Cain and Abel heard God speak to them individually. Abraham heard the voice of God when he promised an heir and another time when he was told to sacrifice his promised son.

God spoke to Moses through a burning bush after being in the desert for 40 years herding sheep. God called out to Samuel four times in the middle of the night when he was a child. In later years, God told Samuel where to find and anoint the first two kings of Israel. The Lord sent Nathan to King David to confront him regarding his sin against God. He had committed adultery with another man's wife and then had her husband sent to the front lines of a battle so that he would be killed. God spoke through another person due to the sin in David's life.

The Lord appeared to young King Solomon during the night in a dream, and God said, "Ask for whatever you want me to give you." Solomon asked for a discerning heart to rule over God's people. God told him that due to his unselfish heart he would give him the discerning heart as well as honor and riches.

The people of Israel were promised that God would be with them, and He spoke to them. They won victory in many battles that they had encountered.

The weeping prophet Jeremiah heard the voice of God several times while the people of Israel were in captivity in Babylon. There were several documented scriptures where it is stated, "This is what the Lord has said." Read Jeremiah 29: 11-14 and see if you witness how encouraging these words were spoken by God to His people.

What about the New Testament scriptures? God spoke through His son, Jesus Christ. Jesus spoke the very words of God the Father because He was God in the flesh. Jesus taught the penetrating sermon on the mountaintop as he sat speaking to a large group of people. He walked among the people healing, touching individual lives and speaking in the temple. He sat down privately with His twelve disciples to speak to them about the kingdom of God.

Jesus would die on a cruel cross for humanity because God the Father required a pure blood sacrifice for the redemption of sin. We become righteous before a Holy God when we accept this precious sacrifice by faith.

Jesus promised to send the comforter in the form of the Holy Spirit when He passed on to paradise to remind us of everything that He had said. The Holy Spirit was received with full power on the day of Pentecost and remains active for all generations to receive as a gift from God the Father. The Holy Spirit is received when we have faith in the truth of what Jesus Christ did on the cross and believe in His resurrection.

What are some of the ways that the Holy Spirit may speak to us in the time that we live? It is simply a whisper, and you can learn to listen for the still small voice of God. The words penned in this book are very personal and real for this author. She hopes that it will open your heart to some avenues that God may express Himself through the power of the Holy Spirit. My hope and desire is for you to become more sensitive to God's activity through, around and in your life. May the Lord touch your heart in ways you never thought possible.

I want to thank the City of Westport, Washington, for the quiet surrounding atmosphere in which to write. I was able to focus on the Lord and be still in His presence. I want to thank Susy Jacobs, Nadine Richmond, Jacky Hornady, Julie Woolsey and Wayne Gundersen for their gentle encouragement. May the Lord bless you. I want to thank my precious husband, Rev. Martin Nordloh, for his belief in me as a woman of faith. Listen for the still small voice of God.

I want to thank Jacky Hornady, Don Tannehill and Mary Jacobson for their work in reading and editing this book.

CHAPTER 1

The Whisper Sings
through Nature

D oes God speak today? Could God be whispering today? Maybe God whispers to our hearts in a variety of ways to draw you close to Him. The Bible tells us that in the beginning He created the mountains, the oceans, the plant life and animal life. Have you been to the Grand Canyon and stood on the edge looking down into the canyon, or have you been to the Bryce Canyon where the monuments are many like large spirals that reach to the sky, in Utah? The fingers of God carved these two canyons out so totally different. Have you ever driven through the winding roads of South Carolina, North Carolina and Virginia? Have you seen or been to the Alps of Switzerland or stood on a mountaintop covered in snow? The experience of flying in a plane to witness the beauty of the Alaskan wilderness can be amazing! Have you seen the dance of the aurora borealis in the night sky? Have you visited and looked at the red mountains in Sedona, Arizona? How many of you have stood on the shorelines of Georgia, California, Washington, Oregon, Hawaii or Italy to view the ocean? Have you have been on a cruise out in the middle of the ocean and what did you witness? Have you ever walked the Great Wall of China? You sometimes can be driving under a canopy of trees that shadows your automobile with beams of sunlight flickering through

1

the trees. Have you seen documentaries showing you the many wonders of nature in the world? Have you seen pictures that try to capture the view of these wonders? Has your mind been drawn to the realization that there is a God that created all the beauty that you have seen? When you know without a doubt that God created what you have seen, then that was His whisper to you that He is real! He sings through the wonders of nature.

It seems the rivers, the trees, the rocks, the oceans and the seas clap their hands together in a symphony of praise to God! (Psalms 98:8) The sun, the moon and the stars reflect the wonder of the Creator of heaven and earth. (Psalms 148:3-4) The mountains and hills burst into song as we witness the Glory of God. (Isaiah 55:12)

God created the foundations of the earth and marked off its dimensions. (Job 38:4-7) God spoke to Job, in his distress, to reveal how He was there to create all of nature and the universe. God told Job that the angels shouted for joy!

> *Psalms 95:3-7, For the Lord is the great God, the great King above all gods. In his hand are the depths of the earth, and the mountain peaks belong to him. The sea is his, for he made it, and his hands formed the dry land. Come, let us bow down in worship, let us kneel before the Lord our Maker; for he is our God and we are the people of his pasture, the flock under his care. NIV*

The voice of the Lord is over all that He created, and He sings the thunder in rhythm as He brings the rains to nourish the lands. The Lord's voice is powerful! (Psalms 29:3-9) In the New Testament Jesus spoke in parables to teach the people the truth of what God wanted them to know. (Note: A parable is a short story that the people could easily relate to, and it had a deeper spiritual meaning. People who were sensitive to God would pick up on it, but those who were not, just heard a story.) He wanted the people to stay close to Him, to learn of Him and be like Him. He would often use nature to bring out a deeper understanding.

John 15:5, "I am the vine; you are the branches. If a man remains in me and I in him, he will bear much fruit; apart from me you can do nothing. NIV

Jesus taught about the kingdom of God by using something they understood. The mustard seed is the smallest seed that grows to become a giant tree. The people understood what He was talking about because Jesus was planting His seed of truth in their hearts so that it could grow through these wise messages. The people that listened and applied His teaching to their lives would one day draw others to the truth of His testimony through them. This is how the kingdom would grow.

Luke 13:18-19, Then Jesus asked, "What is the kingdom of God like? What shall I compare it to? It is like a mustard seed, which a man took and planted in his garden. It grew and became a tree, and the birds of the air perched in its branches." NIV

Nature whispers to our hearts! The flowers need the rain to help them grow, so God allows the rain of tribulation to assist us to grow. God sends the sunshine to our hearts so that we can experience His love.

Jesus spoke about how and why He would die. He shared how the wheat seed must die so that the wheat would grow. (John 12:23-25) He spoke about the heart of a man and how many ways people would respond to His teachings. The seed was the Word of God. The seed would fall on a dry surface, on rocky ground, in the weeds and on good ground. Read (Matthew 13:18-23) for the explanation.

Please continue to read the rest of this chapter so that you can capture more of how nature could whisper to you. Put yourself in the picture.

The Sunrise in the Morning

When driving to work in Enid, Oklahoma from Nash, Oklahoma, the sun would often be rising and this scenery would prompt me to pray. The prayers would often start with acknowledging His presence in praise. Praising Him for the paintbrush sunrises that He gifts me to witness. The sky would be filled with the color of orange, flowing white clouds and streams of yellow. Sometimes a small cloud would appear that would grow larger until it appeared to cover the sun. Then the sun's rays would appear from all sides shooting down to the earth. The sky was filled with the artistry of the Creator of the Universe. It was almost felt like the sky was praising God, as the view would become more and more majestic. Sunrise artist tapestries from God's paintbrush are never the same. The clouds appeared to look like a quilt with rows of gray rolling circles, or pillows of white fluff scattered everywhere. There were vast differences in each sunrise that was created, and these expressions of God's love did not just happen.

Thanking Him for so many blessings that are not bought with money: the air we breathe, a country where we can live freely to Worship Him, the church Marty and I served in, the people that we had grown to love so very much, the good health we were experiencing, two grown children who have surrendered to His love. The love that comes from God is powerful, and there is no comparison. I have a parent's love, but not a complete and accepting love (Agape) that the Holy Spirit gives to His children. God's love is offered freely to the people that have surrendered to being observant and sensitive to the Lord living through their life.

During the winter it became very dark driving to work. The stars were still in the sky, fading quickly as the sunrise brightened the sky as the drive continued when suddenly the words coming from my heart: "the whisper of God" is present this morning. He brought to my memory about the story of Abraham when He promised him that because he was obedient to the Lord his descendants would outnumber the stars in the sky. Why was Abraham so blessed by God? He grew to have faith and a friendship with the Lord. He knew the whisper of God and became obedient to His requests. The Holy Spirit will bring the Word to our minds as we become more knowledgeable of what God has said through the Bible. Believers are those stars promised to Abraham as we grow in friendship and faith in the Lord who is Sovereign. He is in control of all things that have been created. The sunrise is the beginning of a new day that says "hello" from a God that loves us.

Psalms 19:1-6, The heavens declare the glory of God; the skies proclaim the work of his hands. Day after day they pour forth speech; night after night they display knowledge. There is no speech or language where their voice is not heard. Their voice goes out into all the earth, their words to the ends of the world. In the heavens he has pitched a tent for the sun, which is like a bridegroom coming forth from his pavilion, like a champion rejoicing to run his course. It rises at one end of the heavens and makes its circuit to the other; nothing is hidden from its heart. NIV

The Bald Eagle Chase

Our family was traveling through Montana in our recreational vehicle when we chose to camp near a large flowing river that was surrounded by tall shadowing pine trees. We set up camp settling for the evening, and then we took our lounge chairs to sit by the river. Out of what seemed nowhere a beautiful bald eagle began chasing another smaller eagle for the fish in his claws; the two birds flew down through a riverbed in front of our view. Up and down, back and forth, the smaller eagle with the fish was being chased while making loud screeching noises. The smaller eagle did not want to let go of the fish in its claws. We watched as the bald eagle pursued in beautiful aerial slides through the sky. These gorgeous birds passed by where we were sitting several times until the smaller eagle let the fish go. The bald eagle scooped up the fish and flew out of sight within seconds. The beauty, strength and power of seeing a bald eagle in flight was breath-taking. I can understand first hand what makes the bald eagle so majestic as my eyes watched how powerful this bird was in flight!

The Spirit of God reminded me that we are to mount up like eagles and fly with confidence in this world. The simple whisper of the Holy Spirit speaks through nature if we take time to listen. We have the same power as the bald eagle as we become completely trusting in the power of the Holy Spirit that lives in us as believers.

Isaiah 40:31 "… those who hope in the Lord will renew their strength. They will soar on wings like eagles; they will run and not grow weary, they will walk and not be faint." NIV

Low Tides

Have you ever stood at the ocean edge watching the waves hit the shoreline early in the morning? My husband's parents have lived in Westport, Washington, for more than thirty-five years. This small community is due west of Olympia, Washington. We were told by one of the local residents to go out early on a specified morning to watch the tide moving because the tide is the lowest on this particular day than any other time of the year. It has been documented that sometimes there may be as many as five extremely low tides in a row in June, from the 13th through the 17th. This is due to the placement of the moon in the atmosphere. She stated that you could walk out for yards and witness ocean life in their natural habitat: the seashells, the sand dollars, sea urchins and much more.

We decided to get up this one morning to watch the tide move out. The morning was overcast but not cold. The moving of the water leaving the shoreline is noticeable, but it does not move very fast. The currents make the water move in rotations as the small waves hit the shoreline over and over in the same pattern. Then more and more of the shoreline is revealed until rocks begin to pop up with the activity of life. The soft sounds of the foghorn are heard bouncing over the ocean from some distance away. No people are seen anywhere because it was too early in the morning. We watched for over an hour allowing our hearts to hear the whisper of God. The ocean sings the message of life. God created the heavens and the earth for us to enjoy. He stated that all what He created was good. There was God's soft symphony of music being played with the rolling of the waves, the foghorn and the chirping of seagulls.

> *Genesis 1:9-13 And God said, "Let the water under the sky be gathered to one place, and let dry ground appear." And it was so. God called the dry ground "land," and the gathered waters he called "seas." And God saw that it was good. Then God said, "Let the land produce vegetation: seed-bearing plants and trees bear fruit with seed in it, according to their various kinds." And it was so. The land produced vegetation: plants bearing seed according to their kinds and trees bearing*

fruit with seed in it according to their kinds. And God saw that it was good. And there was evening, and there was morning — the third day. NIV

The ocean expresses the power of God through the surges of the water rolling to the shoreline every day in all parts of the world. God is everywhere for all men to hear His whispers of nature that He has created. We need to stop what we may be doing, thinking and thank God for all that He has given. Rest in His love.

Snoqualmie Pass and Other Mountains

There was a feeling of being hugged when we drove through the mountains that penetrated the sky on both sides from the Snoqualmie Pass in Washington State. The white fluffy clouds framed the tops of the mountains. The small waterfalls that flowed from the rocks at the side of the road added to the beauty of the landscape. As we drove, we came to the top of the mountain pass, and there was still evidence of the previous snowfall. The green hills and mountains filled the landscape with pine trees and other plant life. The quick view of a deer peeked through the green full brush. What a majestic view of vast high mountain ranges that seemed really to hug us and say, "Have a wonderful day".

While we were driving, we noticed many people in other automobiles stretching their necks to look to the height of the mountain's grandeur as we were doing. God truly has given us His beautiful creation to enjoy. I have driven this mountain pass during the winter, and the snow can bring a much different view of these majestic mountains. They can even become dangerous, as often avalanches will close the roads.

My husband and I would often comment that God truly is the greatest artist and that His glory is revealed all through what He has created! There are other mountain tapestries that God has created all over the world. The mountains in Switzerland, Austria, the Rocky Mountains in Colorado and the mountains all through the State of Oregon, Idaho, Montana, and Wyoming are majestic. The rolling hills in North and South Carolina are beautiful showing how God mastered and planned all that He made. God has taken his creative paintbrushes and painted the hillsides with oranges, yellows, and fire engine reds during the fall seasons in several parts of the world. He whispers His glory in all that He has created. He did this for us to enjoy because He loves His people. The whisper is heard deep within the heart of those that become truly His people, who have accepted His gift of salvation through the sacrifice of God's pure lamb, Christ Jesus.

> *Isaiah 52:7 How beautiful on the mountains are the feet of those who bring good news, who proclaim peace, who bring good tidings, who proclaim salvation, who say to Zion, "Your God reigns!" NIV*

There have been several times that we have driven over the mountain passes in Colorado witnessing that the higher we drove the less plant life was visible. Someone once said that when he was standing on a mountaintop and then looked in a valley, that is where he saw all the plant growth. We do not want to stay on a mountaintop too long because then we will not grow spiritually. It is through the valley of life's suffering that we will hear the whispers of God.

The Power of Waterfalls

On the Island of Maui, Hawaii, there are several cascading waterfalls. There is a long drive to an inactive volcano where these waterfalls are seen. The road is narrow and winding as we continued to climb in elevation. One of the views of a waterfall suddenly appears on the right side of the road. The vegetation is everywhere with palm trees, ferns and green flowing brush all around when we viewed this waterfall that falls high above where we were watching.

We are again reminded that God created this beauty out of an active volcano deep within the ocean that surrounds this island. The whisper of His presence and His glory is experienced.

My husband pastored a church in Chelan, Washington, during his career and was asked to officiate a wedding for a young couple near the small community of Stehekin, Washington. The only way that we could travel to this community was by boat or by hiking. The couple chose to be married near the "Rainbow Falls", which is just beyond Stehekin, Washington. This would mean that the wedding party and their guests would have to hike to the area to be near the "Rainbow waterfall."

When we traveled by boat we experienced cascading mountains on both sides from Lake Chelan to Stehekin and this ride is about two hours long. The "Rainbow Falls" has been the background view of many beautiful weddings.

Why would people choose to have this kind of experience to begin their life together? This nature experience reminds me of the setting when a man and a woman were first created. God created the Garden of Eden for Adam and Eve, which could have been much like some of natural gardens we view in areas that I have just described. The beautiful original home that God created for men and women to live in was closed to them once the sin of disobedience occurred. Human beings were then told to work for their living by God. We cause our own problems a great deal of the time.

The power of water cascading down the side of a tall mountain reminds me also of the power of God in our lives as believers. A waterfall seems to never have an ending source of water supply. Again, I am reminded of Scripture in the Bible. Jesus is the living water where we never will thirst again. His wisdom could be compared to the power of each droplet of water that forms in the waterfall, because it is ongoing forever and forever. Jesus spoke to a Samaritan woman at a well just outside of the town of Sychar about the living water that he would give to those who would believe in Him.

> *John 4:7-14, A woman of Samaria came to draw water. Jesus said to her, "Give Me a drink." For His disciples had gone away into the city to buy food. Then the woman of Samaria said to Him, "How is it that You, being a Jew, ask a drink from me, a Samaritan woman?" For Jews have no dealings with Samaritans. Jesus answered and said to her, "If you knew the gift of God, and who it is who says to you, 'Give Me a drink,' you would have asked Him, and He would have given you living water." The woman said to Him, "Sir, You have nothing to draw with, and the well is deep. Where then do You get that living water? Are You greater than our father*

> *Jacob, who gave us the well, and drank from it himself, as well as his sons and his livestock?" Jesus answered and said to her, "Whoever drinks of this water will thirst again, but whoever drinks of the water that I shall give him will never thirst. But the water that I shall give him will become in him a fountain of water springing up into everlasting life." NKJV*

God loves by allowing the beautiful whisper in the power of a waterfall to speak of the glory of His presence to our life. We will never thirst again if we accept the living water that Jesus offers to humanity.

The Changes of Weather through the Seasons

The seasons of winter, spring, summer and fall are different in all areas of the world. The season of winter sometimes brings the experience of snow, wind, freezing rain and lower temperatures. The season of spring brings the gift of new animal life, new plant life from the ground, sometimes tornadoes, warmer temperatures, rain, thunderstorms and late frost. The summer season sometimes brings us the higher temperatures, the longer days, the gentle breezes, the rains that water the earth, hurricanes and plant life in full bloom. The fall sometimes brings us the change of colors in the trees, the beginning of lower temperatures, animal life starting to prepare for a winter's sleep, like the bear, and early snow. These seasons are different all over the world. For instance in Egypt it maybe the winter season and it is warm. Alaska's winter season has much shorter days than the lower forty-eight states. The summer season has longer daylight hours. There are often earthquakes that shake the earth in Alaska, California, Washington and other parts of the world during any season of the year.

We can then go beyond the earth and learn about how God balances the Universe by creating other planets, the stars, the sun and the moons. The moon that is close to the earth draws the high and low tides of the oceans to the shorelines. The earth's position to the sun brings us our weather through the seasons of every year. These events just did not happen out of nowhere. The mastermind of the Great Creator placed all the seasons and the weather in position. God gave humanity all this to enjoy because He loves so passionately.

God does allow destruction to happen. The rain does fall on the just and unjust alike, though. He is in control of all seasons and the weather.

Throughout the Old Testament as I have read about the character of God, I have learned what He does not like in us. He does not like grumbling, disrespect for His chosen leaders, disobedience to His direct commands and placing other gods or idols before him that replace our love and relationship with Him. We go through the seasons of disobedience and obedience as we live as believers. He allows the rains, thunderstorms, and the hurricanes of discipline to fall on us when it is needed for our growth. God reminds us that He is in control and that man created nothing that is living.

The thunderstorms make crashing sounds and the lighting streaks across the sky and then there is a pattering sound of the rain. This reminds me about the thunderstorms that do happen in our lives. The rain reminds me of the Savior's cleansing power. After the storm a brilliant rainbow appears in the sky. The God of the Universe whispers the same message from the sky that He did when He placed the rainbow in the sky. He made humanity a promise. He would no longer flood the entire earth and destroy all living creatures. His purpose for destroying the entire earth's life is because the people had become disobedient and He only found one man who was faithful.

> *Genesis 9:12-16, And God said, "This is the sign of the covenant I am making between me and you and every living creature with you, a covenant for all generations to come: I have set my rainbow in the clouds, and it will be the sign of the covenant between me and the earth. Whenever I bring clouds over the earth and the rainbow appears in the clouds, I will remember my covenant between me and you and all living creatures of every kind. Never again will the waters become a flood to destroy all life. Whenever the rainbow appears in the clouds, I will see it and remember the everlasting covenant between God and all living creatures of every kind on the earth." NIV*

The life of a human being allows people to live through the season of new birth, the season of childhood, the seasons of being a young and then an older adult. I am thankful to the Lord that God has granted me all these seasons of life. To live my life in obedience to the Lord is my greatest prayer, but I have and will fail from time to time to be all that I could be in Jesus Christ. We should be thankful that Jesus Christ has provided for us His forgiveness when we fail to do what is right in His eyes. The Old Testament repeated over and over the willingness for God to forgive man if He returned to being obedient to His commands and renewing our relationship with Him.

The seasons of life bring victory but then we may run in fear for our life. When standing on a mountain ridge of the Grand Canyon in Arizona, the Holy Spirit brought to my mind the story of Elijah when He confronted the people of Israel regarding their sins of serving false gods. He asked King Ahab to bring the priests of these false gods and meet him at Mt Carmel. The true God of Abraham, Isaac and Jacob revealed Himself powerfully through the obedience of the prophet Elijah. He was willing to be the instrument where God was glorified. His life was threatened after this powerful victory, and then he ran. He grumbled to the Lord finding himself in a cave at Mt. Horeb, the mountain of God. Read what happened with Elijah.

> *1 Kings 19:9-12 "There he went into a cave and spent the night. And the word of the Lord came to him: 'What are you doing here, Elijah?' He replied, 'I have been very zealous for the Lord God Almighty. The Israelites have rejected your covenant, broken down your altars, and put your prophets to death with the sword. I am the only one left, and now they are trying to kill me too.' The Lord said, 'Go out and stand on the mountain in the presence of the Lord, for the Lord is about to pass by. Then a great and powerful wind tore the mountains apart and shattered the rocks before the Lord, but the Lord was not in the wind. After the wind there was an earthquake, but the Lord was not in the earthquake. After the earthquake came a fire, but the Lord was not in the fire. And after the fire came a gentle whisper." NIV*

Elijah received his final instructions from the whisper of God and became obedient to the Lord's commands.

The Holy Spirit of God whispers to us through seasons of weather and through the seasons of our life. We need to remember that the scriptures told Elijah that He was not in the wind, earthquake and the fire, but in a gentle whisper following the fire. We sometimes are not willing to listen until a fire passes through our life. We need to be still and know that He is God. He may just whisper your name.

The Meadows of Green Pastures

In the spring of every year through the world there is the beginning of new growth. Flowers appear, trees bud blossoms and the meadows are ripe with green grass. You begin to see new birth in the animal world like fawns, bunnies, bear cubs and the bald eagles nesting.

Have you ever run through the tall grass in a field? You may have taken your shoes off after a beautiful lawn has just been mowed? You may be thankful that winter was finally over, even when it may have been harsh; there is new life that appears. God has a message for all humanity in the spring of all of our lives. There needs to be another reminder to "Be still and know He is God." Make the time to praise and thank the Lord for the beauty of the soft meadow your bare feet are touching. When you drive past new growth of wheat fields and view the green meadows everywhere, thank the Lord for food being produced. Pray for the farmers that work hard in those fields, but without God's rain, the field would never grow. Man truly needs God. God's power is witnessed because all plant, animal life and meadows continue to thrive with His creative touch.

The stream that flows through a meadow can be a wonderful place where you can sit and read your Bible. The whisper of God through nature is present wherever, or whenever, you chose to take time to rest and listen.

> *Psalms 23:1-3, "The Lord is my shepherd; I shall not be in want. He makes me lie down in green pastures, he leads me beside quiet waters, he restores my soul. He guides me in paths of righteousness for his name's sake." NIV*

1. *Pray:*

Lord, open my heart and eyes to see your beauty of your creation around me. Help me to understand how much you reflect your love in what you have created. Help me to listen for your whispers through nature. Amen

2. *Reflection:*

Have you experienced the presence of God through nature? If you have, would you be willing to express what you felt? Where was the nature experience located? How special did it make you feel?

CHAPTER 2

The Whisper in Prayer

N ow that you are beginning to relax in the Lord you could be recognizing God's presence. You may be experiencing your own gifts through nature that God has given to you. My prayer is that you find His peace that He alone can give you. My Pastor Brother and I were speaking one day about some of his experiences with the whispers God has given him through nature. He walked up a hill on the Golden Gate Baptist Theological seminary Campus and began to look on to the Golden Gate Bridge. He watched the activity of the boats, the cars passing over the bridge and the majestic flow of the water under the bridge. He was seeking God's peace and directions for the ministry the Lord had called him to do. The setting was perfect for him to begin to pray. Viewing this scenery for this day became his personal prayer closet. This was peaceful for him, and the presence of the Lord was profoundly present. He continued to pray for a long time opening his heart to the Lord. God's whispers began to fill his heart and to give him peace regarding what direction the Lord was leading. Prayer is what changes our hearts. He heard the whisper that gave him what he had desired.

This chapter will be directing you through more of how God whispers to us, as believers, in prayer. We are asked by Jesus Christ to find a private place where we can pray and be still enough to hear His whispers back to us.

> *Matthew 6:5-6, "And when you pray, do not be like the*
> *hypocrites, for they love to pray standing in the synagogues*
> *and on the street corners to be seen by men. I tell you the*
> *truth; they have received their reward in full. But when*
> *you pray, go into your room, close the door and pray to your*
> *Father, who is unseen." NIV*

The Joy of Peace

What is peace? As a little girl I thought peace was having no wars in the world and no fighting with neighbors, siblings or friends. Peace to me meant that everybody would be happy all the time! These were natural thoughts coming from a child, but maybe that is what you would call peace. Until we truly repent, receiving Jesus Christ as our personal Savior there can be no real peace. There will still be wars, rumors of war, violence and still have arguments with our neighbors, siblings or friends, but we will be able to find the peace that comes from the Lord in having a relationship with Him. The need for you to argue will become less and less as you surrender to the Lord Jesus Christ in prayer. The Holy Spirit manifests Himself through your mortal bodies and minds, as believers.

The peace that you receive as you pray will be an ongoing experience every time you humble yourselves to communicating with the Lord. This morning, as these words are written, I am having an open dialogue with Him. What is it that He wants to be said? He whispers His peace of approval as I give Him the right to express Himself to me with His whisper through my heart. He wants you to have His peace. He will never ask us to do something that does not include some kind of interaction with other people because it is what will further and strengthen His kingdom. Your lives are to be open books to the world so that God is magnified. He is alive and should be glorified as the one true God that is worshiped. He is so willing to forgive us if you would just turn your hearts back to Him. We all have become a stiff-necked people that have become too busy to communicate to the Lord or give Him much time through prayer. His peace is waiting for you if you only surrender to being in His presence. This statement may be harsh, but this is what it will take to find the joy of peace that only comes from the Holy Spirit through prayer. How do you begin your prayer to Him? You first acknowledge Him with a humble heart addressing Him in awe of whom you are communicating with and then you can speak your praises. Your personal concerns should be last during our prayer time. We are a people that pray for ourselves most of the time, and then we wonder why there is no peace in our prayers. The self-centered prayers are heard, but how can we ever hear His whispers of peace to our hearts if we are not focused on who we are talking to? He will bless us through prayer revealing that it is a gift to be in communication with the Almighty God. Don't you suppose He sees your heart's condition before you begin to pray? The joy of peace comes from allowing God to whisper to your heart as He has chosen to do. Please allow Him to have His way with your heart, be open to hearing His whispers and then you will grow to becoming more and more familiar to when God is speaking through prayer.

Several years ago a book was published called the "The Jabez Prayer," and this changed my life of prayer. I accepted the challenge to read this little book every day for thirty days submitting to what God wanted to say to me. (Note: The challenge was to read it every week for thirty days.) This became a springboard model prayer like the "Lord's Prayer" has been to sometimes start my prayers. The Lord's Prayer has taught us to acknowledge God first, "Hallowed be Thy Name."

> *Matthew 6:9-13, "This, then, is how you should pray: 'Our Father in heaven, hallowed be your name, your kingdom come, your will be done on earth as it is in heaven. Give us today our daily bread. Forgive us our debts, as we also have forgiven our debtors. And lead us not into temptation; but deliver us from the evil one.'" NIV*

This next prayer is a sample that has been prayed using the Lord's Prayer as a model:

> "Father, your name is above all names; you are majestic, powerful, loving and full of wisdom. Lord, praying for a spiritual revival for our world, so that your kingdom will

be revealed like it is in heaven. Lord, I ask you to provide for my family and meet our needs as we live this day out. Teach us your Word, so that we can grow strong in our faith. Help me to forgive others like you have forgiven me. Keep the enemy away from my heart and the doorstep of my home. In Jesus' Name, Amen"

These model prayers are wonderful outlines of how you can begin to pray to find that peace that the Holy Spirit wants to give you. These model prayers allow God to have His way through and in your prayer life.

The prayer using the Jabez prayer as a model may start, "Lord God Almighty, bless me, so that I may glorify you, enlarge my territory of influence so that the truth of God's love can be revealed through this servant. Without your hand upon my heart I will not be able to express the message of salvation through Jesus Christ clearly. Lord, I will need your protection from the lies of the enemy and am asking for healing to my body so that others will witness your grace."

These prayers are just a couple of samples of how God has used them to work in my life.

> *1 Chronicles 4:9-10, "Jabez was more honorable than his brothers. His mother had named him Jabez, saying, 'I gave birth to him in pain.' Jabez cried out to the God of Israel, "Oh, that you would bless me and enlarge my territory! Let your hand be with me, and keep me from harm so that I will be free from pain.' And God granted his request." NIV*

Scripture in Prayer

There may be times that when you desire to do something for the Lord that is misinterpreted by other well-meaning believers. This is the best time to pray and ask for God's understanding and perspective on a matter that is concerning you. The Lord will whisper to you with scripture at times. This next scripture is one that gives God's perspective about believers that may have a difference of opinion. There will be times when your heart's motives are not according to God's will either. You may want to ask yourself if you are attempting to get personal attention.

> *Romans 14:1-12, Receive one who is weak in the faith, but not to disputes over doubtful things. For one believes he may eat all things, but he who is weak eats only vegetables. Let not him who eats despise him who does not eat, and let not him who does not eat judge him who eats; for God has received him. Who are you to judge another's servant? To his own master he stands or falls. Indeed, he will be made to stand, for God is able to make him stand. One person esteems one day above another; another esteems every day alike. Let each be fully convinced in his own mind. He who observes the day, observes it to the Lord; and he who does not observe the day, to the Lord he does not observe it. He who eats, eats to the Lord, for he gives God thanks; and he who does not eat, to the Lord he does not eat, and gives God thanks. For none of us lives to himself, and no one dies to himself. For if we live, we live to the Lord; and if we die, we die to the Lord. Therefore, whether we live or die, we are the Lord's. For to this end Christ died and rose and lived again, that He might be Lord of both the dead and the living. But why do you judge your brother? Or why do you show contempt for your brother? For we shall all stand before the judgment seat of Christ. For it is written: "As I live, says the Lord, Every knee shall bow to Me, And every tongue shall confess to God." So then each of us shall give account of himself to God. NKJV*

You must realize that each person is accountable to God and not to man. When the Holy Spirit reveals the desire of God on an appointment that He wants you to follow through with, He will join you in the activity. This way, God will be glorified. Waiting for God's fullness of time on a matter is a learning process and so is listening for His whispers. You truly learn this through spending time in prayer.

The scriptures can also be repeated as a prayer to God. You can place your name in the areas that may say 'whosoever' in the Word. The scriptures speak to us as the Holy Spirit interprets them to our heart, but they can bless the Lord's heart as you repeat them back to Him in communication. Your heart then speaks back to Him. You can read scriptures as a prayer to the Lord. The Book of Psalms are excellent scriptures to pray. You simply need to be open to hearing the whispers of God that come from the Holy Spirit as you pray. Here is an example that could encourage you by reading the following scripture that was expressed by King David. If you feel the same way with the words David prayed, then they can become your own words to God.

> *I Chronicles 29: 10-13, "David (You praise in like manner) praised the Lord in the presence of the whole assembly, saying, 'Praise be to you, O Lord, God of our father Israel, from everlasting to everlasting. Yours, O Lord, is the greatness and the power and the glory and the majesty and the splendor, for everything in heaven and earth is yours. Yours, O Lord, is the kingdom; you are exalted as head over all. Wealth and honor come from you; you are the ruler of all things. In your hands are strength and power to exalt and give strength to all. Now, our God, we give you thanks, and praise your glorious name.'" NIV*

God's Divine Love

There were experiences when we were children that we may have feared punishment when we did something wrong. Have you ever stewed about the kind of discipline you were going to receive? You knew that you had made a big mistake, so unwieldy thoughts of fear knowing you would have to tell your parents filled your mind.

Three teenagers were driving the back roads of a town in Colorado. The oldest teenager was 18 years old, who was driving her parent's car, allowed her 15-year-old brother to get in the driver's seat. He had just received his learner's permit and she wanted him to get some experience driving on these quiet back roads. There was no traffic seen any where, so her younger brother started up the car and when he released the break the car slide right in the ditch along the deserted road. There was no way that the car could be driven out of the ditch without a tow truck. Her brother's friend suggested that they all walk to the closest farmhouse to call for help. All three teenagers got out of the car and started walking towards the house. It was dark and the road was hard to follow, but they walked on with the house in view. They were getting close to the house and turned to see another car pull up to their car that was in the ditch. They thought that help had come, so the two boys started running back to the car. Several gunshots were heard and then the other car drove away.

The teenage girl began running towards the farmhouse to get help. A lady at the house opened the door, but would not let the teenage girl in her home. She agreed to call her parents and the police. The girl heard the footsteps of the boys running towards the house, too. They all waited outside in the dark for the parents and the police to arrive. The sun was beginning to rise and the dusk of daylight was rising to see the approaching police and the teenager's parents. The two vehicles were parked near the car in the ditch, so all three teenagers started to walk towards the cars. When girl walked up to the car and looked at the damage to the car in the ditch. The windows were all shot out and the seats in the car had bullet holes in them. The police said, "We are thankful that none of you kids remained in the car." He said that this was a random shooting and they may never find the perpetrators. The parents were thankful all the teenagers were unharmed. The teenagers were forgiven and punishment was not given to any of them due to the trauma they had already experienced. Everyone believed that the Lord allowed the car to slide into the ditch to get the kids out of the car, so that they would not be shooting victims. There were mistakes made on that road that night, but it could have been a tragedy. I am sure those teenagers thought they would be punished until the end of time, or maybe even be taken to jail.

Sometimes you do things and have thoughts that you feel that you should be disciplined for because you have learned what God has expected of you by reading the word. You wait in fear in what you think needs to happen and then it does not happen. You sometimes take charge of your own discipline with thoughts that are harmful. You need see yourself as a person that is worth loving and forgiven. When you live in the flesh, you sometimes serve the desires of the flesh that may harm your witness as a believer. We were all born sinful accept for one solitary life of Jesus Christ.

When you make mistakes that are in contradiction with what the Bible tells us to do, you must repent. You might have to ask God to change YOUR ATTITUDE. You then leave God in charge of what happens next. He loves a heart that is sorry for the sin(s) you fight with doing every day. He does whisper His Divine Love towards you as you pray for forgiveness.

> *Isaiah 55:7-9 "Let the wicked forsake his way and the evil man his thoughts. Let him turn to the Lord, and he will have mercy on him, and to our God, for he will freely pardon. 'For my thoughts are not your thoughts, neither are your ways my ways,' declares the Lord. 'As the heavens are higher than the earth, so are my ways higher than your ways and my thoughts than your thoughts'". NIV*

Time spent in prayer leads to words directed by the Holy Spirit. You may ask yourself, "How much time should I spend in Prayer?" Your first prayer as a child may have been "Now I lay me down to sleep." This is a model prayer that sometimes may have ended with God bless Mom, God bless Dad, God bless everyone that is on your personal list. Your prayers may have been very short and others may have gone on and on. A 3-year-old boy we knew once would often pray at the dinner table. His parents would sometimes ask to him to lead the prayer. He would ask everyone to repeat after him as he prayed. If he made a mistake, he would start over again asking everyone again to repeat after him. His prayers were sometimes very long. This young couple was willing to teach their child to pray. He truly learned to communicate with the Lord very young.

Some people can speak to God for a long time publicly because they have grown to have a relationship with God. Some people cannot pray publicly at all. Would this mean that they do not have a relationship with the Lord through prayer? My opinion is that when, where and the length of a prayer is neither right nor wrong and is very personal. We need to pray long enough to hear the whisper of God that communicates back to our hearts. The whispers may come back to you during your time with the Lord or later after the prayer. The small, still voice of God will bring thoughts to you that you may never have considered when you pray expecting a two-way communication. Prayer should not be only the sound of your own voice.

When practicing music, I often go to the Lord in prayer because the music is sometimes my private prayer to Him. We are instructed to go into a private room to pray. God has opened my heart to the music choice that glorifies Him. We must sometimes praise Him, acknowledge His presence and then wait for the Holy Spirit's prompting. The prayers can be personal and with a purpose for the circumstances. The Holy Spirit will give me peace and joy in the message of a song that was right for this time of ministry.

A friend of mine was spending time in prayer when she asked God, "Lord, am I praying the right way?" She shared that the words came to her mind, "There is no wrong way to pray." She was focused on the Lord and not on herself, so she heard His whisper.

> *Philippians 4:5-7, "Do not be anxious about anything, but in everything, by prayer and petition, with thanksgiving, present your requests to God. And the peace of God, which transcends all understanding, will guard your hearts and your minds in Christ Jesus." NIV*

The Small Voice of God in One or Two Words

Have you ever been asked to express what you wanted in two or three words? We are a people of many words. There has been a saying that God gave people two ears and one mouth, so that must mean that we are to listen twice as much as we talk. Gary Smalley has written in books and spoken in his seminars that girls know how to speak in full sentences at a young age and that the boys may only say a few words. In fact, all they do is make car engine noises. This was proven when witnessing our two children growing up. Our son did not speak a full sentence until he was about four years old. Doctors were beginning to become concerned because he was not talking very much. He would play for hours with his matchbox cars on the floor. Our daughter was born three years later, and she was speaking full sentences when she was fifteen months old. She drove me crazy walking around following me everywhere in the house, chattering. We sometimes are just talkers, and we do not listen.

My father was excellent at listening. He would stop whatever he was doing to listen to my siblings or my conversations. He was always interested in what we wanted to talk about. He was a very wise man with years of learning to listen because he had been a public school teacher and college professor. His instructions to us were usually in the form of a question so that we would make our own decisions on any given matter. He gently taught us to think for ourselves and then prompted us to take action on the decisions we made. He would say just few words like "Did you get the results you wanted?" or, "What would you do different next time to get a more positive outcome?"

When you begin to pray long enough for the Lord to impress His whispers in the prayers, you may sometimes hear only one, two or three words that interrupt your thinking. The words are usually not in the direction our minds and mouth are talking. The words are expressed with authority, and you know this must be the still, small voice of God. The first time that I experienced this was when the thought popped in my head: "You are special". The surprise of this phrase became emotional and very touching. The Divine love that only the Holy Spirit generates through a believer in Jesus Christ is difficult to explain. The Holy Spirit impresses Himself very effectively with the authority of God when it is needed. You may say to yourself, "This has never happened to me." You need to pray long enough to allow God the opportunity to impress His words back to you. I have heard my pastor husband say, "Praying is much like breathing; you breathe out and then you breathe in". When you are continuously breathing out your own words, you cannot do it very long. When you stop to listen for the whispers of God, you may experience His two or three words that have been meant for you. The Word of God tells us to be still and know that He is God.

I want to make it very clear to you that it will always be God's-choice as to when He will speak to you this way. You cannot force God to give you an experience like this with your own desire and pressure. He will choose the time, the place and the circumstance when it is needed to grow you spiritually. We just need to be open and trusting to His plan working through our life.

> *Psalms 119:130, "The unfolding of your words gives light; it gives understanding to the simple." NIV*

Expressing praise to the Lord that gives us life

There have been many books written regarding the need for praising the Lord. The most prominent book, in the Bible, are the documented praises written by King David and his music leader. These praises are found in the book of Psalms. I know that when I first began to learn to pray I was not praising God at all. I just started speaking like I had the right to pray about anything. It was much like a bull crashing into a cabinet. My prayers were self-centered in the approach to God and I was always asking God for something that I wanted. Have you ever noticed that public prayers in a prayer meeting setting are mostly for the sick in the church family? We are a people who do not reverence the Lord in our prayers. Sometimes prayers are thoughts of telling God what we want to do and asking Him to back us up as we move forward. We want Him to be with us in what we want to do for Him. His answer may be "no". There is a popular song by Garth Brooks called "Thank God for Unanswered Prayers". Do we thank the Lord for unanswered prayers? We should thank the Lord for many unanswered prayers because when we look back we will see that what we really wanted would have been very damaging to us, to our families or to the circumstances that was happening at the time. We must ask ourselves this question, "Would what I am praying for be glorifying to the Lord, or edifying myself?" When we read the testimonies of the people in the Bible, we can recognize that they were human just like we are. They made bad choices, sinned, moved on with their own plans and failed to gain victory that they had hoped would happen. The problem is that they did not wait for the plan that the Lord had in mind for them to do or to make the choice to grow into a deeper relationship with Him.

Stop and think more positively about your communications you have with the Lord. Praise Him for the life witness, words and the ultimate action that Jesus Christ willingly took so that you could live in relationship with Him. You can boldly come, in prayer, to the throne of God with your praises. His final physical action of choosing to die as the perfect sacrifice was provided for you so that you could become the people of God in Jesus Christ that would assist in furthering His kingdom. We must rise above the worries, disappointments, depressions and the cruelty we experience living in the world. You should praise Jesus Christ for being the intercessor for you when you do not know what to say, or for standing before God the Father in all His righteousness so that you can be seen as being righteous. This was the ultimate gift to humanity, for at one time in the past, the people of God had to sacrifice hundreds of cattle, goats, sheep, pigeons and follow detailed guidelines that would attempt to make them right before God. You are living in the time of grace and mercy. You should not take this wonderful gift lightly. You need to praise Him for these gifts. Grace is when you receive His blessings at no personal cost to you, and mercy is when you do not receive the punishment that you all deserve. You should praise the Lord for these gifts that we have been given due to the simple act of faith because that is what Jesus Christ's death provided for all who believe. Praise Him and rise up above your circumstances you face daily. Praise Him when you are ill, praise Him when finances are not there for you, praise Him if you are separated from a loved one, praise Him when you have been wrongly accused, praise Him when you have lost a job, and praise Him when all circumstances seem to be perfect. He will lift you up with His love, and you know that He understands. There is nothing that surprises the Lord. Praise the Lord for His blessings and for the gift of life that you have as a believer. You will feel His whisper of acceptance and approval with peace that only He can give.

> *Psalms 30:4-5, "Sing to the Lord, you saints of his; praise his holy name. For his anger lasts only a moment, but his favor lasts a lifetime; weeping may remain for a night, but rejoicing comes in the morning." NIV*

Surrender your heart to the Lord in Prayer

You fight battles every day with attitudes that may keep you from drawing close to the Lord in prayer. There are interruptions that happen where you do not take time to be still or where you cannot be still in His presence. You live busy lifestyles in today's world. My pastor husband has quoted busy meaning "Bent under Satan's yoke". He did not originate this quote, but this is so very true for many of us during our daily living. We surrender to these busy activities rather than surrendering to time in prayer. Let me ask you a question? What do you suppose the enemy of Satan wants to do? You bet, get our eyes and heart off of prayer that would encourage and strengthen your lives. He is a destroyer of your peace and gives you thoughts of destruction and disappointments. I have often asked people if they read their Bible, or pray or maybe asked if they attend church. Their usual answer is, "I really do not have the time for that." You choose your own priorities, and you are missing out on a fuller life. The Lord Jesus is a perfect gentleman, and He allows you to make your own choices. My desire is not to "guilt" you into being close to the Lord, but to encourage you. Life can be more than a baseball game, a football game, school activities, a job, just going to church and other activities that keep us busy. We can get too busy doing church activities and miss out on having a relationship with God through a surrendered prayer life. My pastor husband has said that we sometimes experience too much church and do not spend enough time growing privately in relationship with God. You can miss His whispers to you that would bring you in line with His plan of action. You need not just be doing only, but you need to be surrendered to His will. Yes, you need to be still before the Lord surrendering your hearts to Him in prayer. Making time for this heart activity leaves you open to hearing the whisper that comes from the Holy Spirit of God. There are scriptures that give you the same message regarding your surrendered humility before the Lord and His promise.

> *1 Peter 5:6-7, "Humble yourselves, therefore, under God's mighty hand, that he may lift you up in due time. Cast all your anxiety on him because he cares for you." NIV*

When Believers Pray for You

The prayers that are spoken for others, God hears and answers. His greatest desire is that you reach out in the grace of the Holy Spirit to pray for others in their need. You will witness the power of God. We witnessed a couple once, as they shared, how much of an impact it was to walk up to a person in church to ask for prayer, and they stopped what they were doing to pray for them on the spot. This couple chose to apply this in their lives when people needed prayers. They encountered people on the street, in a restaurant, in the parking lot of shopping center or in church, and prayed as they saw a need. The response to the care of prayer touches people's lives.

The bodies of believers that pray together hear and witness the activity of God. There are church prayer gatherings that have changed the heart of those present and for those they are praying for God to touch regarding their needs. God has whispered in the middle of praying believers.

There is a Bible story written when Peter had been thrown in jail for preaching the Gospel of Jesus Christ. The plan was, sometime in the future, to have Peter killed, so the people prayed. The group of believers prayed all night for Peter's release. (Acts 12:5-14) Peter then came knocking on their door during the night where the believers were gathered together in prayer. What an answer to prayer!

Earlier in our spiritual walk there was a time when a few people, in the church we were attending, decided to pray for a couple that were going to have an abortion. The people that were agreeing to pray decided on a specific time, laying face down on the floor, in each of our individual homes. Within 10 minutes into our prayer time we received a phone call from the couple stating that were not going to get an abortion. The phone began to ring from the people that had agreed to pray stating that they felt that they didn't need to pray anymore! Corporate prayer works and the baby was a boy. He is now serving in the United States Air Force.

The corporate prayer of believers is vital in the body of a church. When you pray together, you begin to love others, as God would have you love. The many prayers and love from my friends and family for me during my breast cancer recovery was the power of strength that gave me God's peace. I thank the Lord Jesus for answered prayer. I know that when people pray for others and when they see their prayers answered, it is a time to praise and give the glory to God.

The more time you spend in prayer to God the more familiar His whispers are recognized. You know when He is prompting you to talk with Him. He wants to share His heart with you. You will grow to understand how deep God's love really is for you, my dear friend.

1. *Pray:*

Lord, I desire to be close to you today and sometimes I do not know what to say. I know that I need to be still long enough to give you the opportunity to speak to me. Guide my thoughts to focus on what you want me to understand. You are wonderful and a glorious Savior who loves me even I do not deserve your love. Help me to be humble before you as I pray today. Amen

2. *Reflection:*

What have you learned about in this chapter? Are there changes you are willing to make to draw you closer to the Lord? How are you going to apply this information you received in this chapter on the whisper of God through pray?

CHAPTER 3

The Whisper of Music

How you are introduced to music is different for everyone. You may have heard music first from a mother, a father, or a grandmother. This is a gift from God that communicates in so many different ways. Music can sooth you in times of loneliness, depression and the uncertainties that you experience in life. Some hospitals offer music therapy to critically ill patients. Through music you experience the joy, peace and hear the whispers that come by the Holy Spirit of God. My prayer is that you continue to learn to recognize the whisper of God through the avenue of music. Music is communication from the writer to the listener. The writer sometimes is a surrendered and humble servant of God that is empowered by the Holy Spirit.

My mother-in-law was asked one time what her experience with music had been and what this had meant to her? She said that music has spoken to her like no other language ever could. She and dad would often play the song "Whispering Hope" together. She would play the piano and dad would play the saw. Yes, you heard me, a saw! He would use a violin bow that flowed across the dull side of the saw and then he would control the movement of the saw with his left thumb and securely tuck the handle under his right leg. He would bounce his right leg and bend the saw to assist in bringing the beautiful music to life. The music that comes from the saw sounds like it could be from a well-trained female soprano vocalist.

Mom asked if the words could be printed to "Whispering Hope" to assist in introducing this chapter to you. She had just been thinking about this book that I am currently writing, and the Lord brought all these memories to her heart regarding this piece of music. God does whisper His hope to our hearts.

"Whispering Hope"

"Soft as the voice of an angel, Breathing a lesson unheard, Hope with a gentle persuasion whispers her comforting word: Wait till the tempest is done, Hope for the sunshine tomorrow, after the shower is gone. If, in the dark of the twilight, Dim be the region afar, Will not the deepening darkness Brighten the glimmering star? Then when the night is upon us, Why should the heart sink away? When the dark midnight is over, Watch for the breaking of day. Hope, as an anchor so steadfast, Rends the dark veil for the soul, Whither the Master has entered, Robbing the grave of its goal. Come then, O come, glad fruition, Come to my sad weary heart; Come, O Thou blest hope of glory, Never, O never depart."

The chorus goes as follows: "Whispering Hope, oh how welcome thy voice, Making my heart in its sorrow rejoice." This song was based on Hebrews 6:19 "We have this hope as an anchor for the soul, firm and secure. It enters the inner sanctuary behind the curtain." NIV

> *Psalms 7:17, "I will give thanks to the Lord because of his righteousness and will sing praise to the name of the Lord Most High." NIV*

The Whisper through Music Teachers

Music teachers are needed as we learn to read music through playing instruments and singing. Music teachers are hired in many public school systems because music has proven to generate interest in learning other subjects being taught. Learning to read music expands our own creativity. Speaking to a CFO of a large business once where he stated that one of the questions he asks in a job interview was "What is your experience with music?" He said that he had received many different answers, but the ones that he hired were people that could read music. He stated that musicians have been proven to acquire better computer skills because it uses the same creativity to understand computer programming. He was also the director of the Symphony Orchestra in the community where he was living.

You probably have had music teachers that you remember that have taught you respect for music or one that revealed your talent and encouraged your growth in a very personal way. Teachers seem to have the ability to see the potential growth of the student. They see what the student could become as they study under their leadership. This is similar to the way Jesus sees your potential as you study His word and begin to do what He has taught you to do. You reap the rewards of lessons learned to develop the desired results. Jesus taught you to become like Him through the teaching and the life style He revealed to humanity when He was walking among men.

The music teacher that was truly treasured by the community where we lived, in Fort Collins, Colorado, was a lady by the name of Kathryn Bauder. She taught in the public school system and then retired to teach private voice lessons. She was a challenging teacher, but she not only taught vocal techniques, but she shared her faith. She worked with me, personally, on the "Lord's Prayer" at every lesson for about three years. Every word had to have a certain sound, resonance and the correct emotion expressed. She once told me that what the Lord gives us a gift we should be willing to develop that gift and give it back to Him. The whisper from the Lord came through Kathryn's expression of her faith who was teaching me about His love. At the same time she taught me how to express my emotion and love for the Lord's music. I often think about her when I hear or sing "The Lord's Prayer." She taught me how to pray with music.

There have been continued music teachers that have inspired my growth in music and in my relationship with the Lord. Being a student at Golden Gate Baptist Theological Seminary and having studied under some wonderful people of faith assisted in my spiritual understanding of God's music. One of the professor's in a music administration class brought two music pieces for us to listen to and then we were to discuss the pros and cons as to whether the music was appropriate for church worship services? The first one was a hard rock instrumental piece, and the other was a classical piece. The discussion was extremely diverse regarding the two pieces of music. He made his point by stating that there needed to be diversity because there are differences of interest in the world today. He stated that we needed to first understand the people that God has called us to minister to and to reach them through the music that would touch their hearts to respond to the Lord. Our personal interests would not always be what would minister to the people. You need to be sensitive to hearing the whisper of the Lord in choices of music that you make, if God ever leads you to be a worship leader.

The next professor that brought a lesson was from a beginning piano class when he asked how many of us beginning piano students were teaching piano? He stated that we needed to learn ABC and then go out and teach ABC. He said that you learn faster when you are teaching what you have learned. Do you suppose this could be applied in what the Holy Spirit is teaching us through the scriptures? Should we all be teaching?

> *2 Tim 3:16-17, "All Scripture is God-breathed and is useful for teaching, rebuking, training in righteousness, so that the man of God may be thoroughly equipped for every good work." NIV*

The joy of the Lord's music is mentioned all through the Word of God. Music is a teaching tool and a gentle whisper from God that can bring the light of the Gospel to an unbelieving heart, a troubled heart and a heart that desires a closer walk with the Lord.

Praise the Lord for teachers who are willing to teach the truth of what is right and encourage their students to be the best that they can be. The Holy Spirit whispers the absolute truth of God's love, and He expresses that truth sometimes through the avenue of MUSIC.

Passion for God's Music

The passion for music has been one of God's ways of sending me a love letter. The love letters of music has touched many hearts in our world, both past and present. The music that has been sung has been my love letters back to Him, either in private or in front of a group of people. There are some songs that have been written that generate this kind of communication. There are many songs of praise that bless the Lord and our hearts join in unity with the one that wrote these words of praise. There are songs that tell the story of one that may be weak in his faith and God reveals His passion that He has for humanity. There are songs of surrendering to the Lord because we desire what He desires. The love letters through the Lord's music can become an intimate prayer of communication that opens our hearts to His message back to us. The power of the Holy Spirit may prompt a whisper that says "You are standing on Holy Ground." I sometimes take my shoes off in humility before the Lord because He is my primary audience. The Lord's approval is what you should desire and not man's approval. Whether you are singing, teaching or praying publicly you should always desire the audience of the Lord and to focus your hearts towards Him in all that you are doing. This can be accomplished successfully if you first spend time in your prayer closets. The prayer closet must be where you and the Lord are the most comfortable and intimate. He then can whisper what He wants to tell you. You are to focus on the Lord and hear His love letters He wants to send to you through music.

Scriptures have been the subjects of many songs written today. "Moses", "He's Alive" and "Mary Did You Know?" The message rings out to glorify God! Many scripture stories have been put to music for children. Children remember the songs of "Zacheus", "Father Abraham" and "Jonah". You can remember the Bible through music sometimes better then reading the Word.

Music Used for Therapy and Recovery

There is now a known fact that music can be therapy for several ailments that people may have today, which does include mental illnesses as well as for those who are critically ill. The Music Therapist is professionally trained to serve in areas for the physically handicapped, emotionally distressed and communication issues for people who cannot express their feelings. Many hospitals have employed a Music Therapist for their trained services like they would a physical therapist. The mental and emotional health of a patient can benefit from a trained Music Therapist. Music will relax a person that has encountered excessive stress in his life, too.

What can we do as believers to help assist in this area? One of my suggestions would be to go to Nursing Homes with God's music where people need the healing from their loneliness. You may be able to provide music to a children's ward in a hospital after getting permission. These are just a couple of suggestions. When you have a person that is ill at home you may consider getting a group together to sing songs to him outside his home and not just go caroling at Christmas. This caroling could be done at any time of the year. Wouldn't that be fun?

There was one time that I took a chance to sing quietly to a member of our church while she was in ICU at a hospital. She was very restless while she was sleeping. Gently singing in a soft voice, a song from our musical that we had been practicing at church, she noticeably started to relax. A nurse stepped in the room, checked the patient, winked at me and then walked out. This lady recovered but did not remember me being there at all. She recovered from her illness. There is healing power in God's music, and the music may have helped her some, to recover.

My daughter had an experience one time where she went to the home of a member of her church who was dying from cancer, and she sang hymns at the request of this woman's husband. She sang these hymns for several hours. She said that she knew her friend heard the music, and she knew that this brought peace to her and her family. My daughter was tired, but this was an experience that she would never regret nor forget. God's music is therapy to the soul, the mind and the body. God whispers His love to people through music. Music can be used by the Holy Spirit to bring recovery, relief and therapy.

The scriptures are full of the ministry of music that the Lord honored. King Saul had been appointed the first king for the Hebrew people. Samuel anointed the first king of Israel at requests that were made by the people, but God made the choice. The Holy Spirit was upon King Saul as long as he was obedient to the Lord's commands. Once the King became disobedient, an evil spirit tormented him. Samuel was called upon once again to anoint a king to follow King Saul, but he was just a shepherd boy named David who also knew how to play the harp. When the evil spirit was tormenting the king, he requested that someone be found to play music with a harp to sooth him.

> *1 Samuel 16:14-23, But the Spirit of the Lord departed from Saul, and a distressing spirit from the Lord troubled him. And Saul's servants said to him, "Surely, a distressing spirit from God is troubling you. Let our master now command your servants, who are before you, to seek out a man who is a skillful player on the harp. And it shall be that he will play it with his hand when the distressing spirit from God is upon you, and you shall be well." So Saul said to his servants, "Provide me now a man who can play well, and bring him to me." Then one of the servants answered and said, "Look, I have seen a son of Jesse the Bethlehemite, who is skillful in playing, a mighty man of valor, a man of war, prudent in speech, and a handsome person; and the Lord is with him." Therefore Saul sent messengers to Jesse, and said, "Send me your son David, who is with the sheep." And Jesse took a donkey loaded with bread, a skin of wine, and a young goat, and sent them by his son David to Saul. So David came to Saul and stood before him. And he loved him greatly, and he became his armorbearer. Then Saul sent to Jesse, saying, "Please let David stand before me, for he has found favor in my sight." And so it was, whenever the spirit from God was upon Saul, that David would take a harp and play it with his hand. Then Saul would become refreshed and well, and the distressing spirit would depart from him. NKJV*

Greg Buchanan plays some of my favorite harp music today. Our family has often sat by a riverbed in our recreational vehicle relaxing to his music, or just sat quietly in our easy chairs just listening for the whispers of God. Whenever you are stressed with some of this world's activities and worries, then just turn those worries off and listen to this harp music, or the quiet music of your choice. This kind of music therapy will calm the stress in your life that could become very dangerous to you. Be still and know that He is God.

God's Music Transforms Hearts

The world is full of absolutely beautiful music that has transformed many hearts. Many choirs throughout many years have presented the great classical music like the "Messiah". Our great Messiah deserves the best to be written about Him and for us to witness this music. There are many modern musicals like *Celebrate Life, God with Us*, and *Experiencing God* that tell the stories of Jesus Christ and how He touches our life with His whispers through this music. New music is being written as the Lord has worked His message through believers that have grown to have deep relationships with the Lord. How can you say that God does not speak to us today? You need to be still and know that He is God. My recommendation is for you to be open to how the Lord wants to bless you personally as you experience His music.

Witnessing people being transformed and then beginning to worship God through His anointed music is amazing. When you are willing to open your heart and relax in the presence of the Lord, you will be able to hear His whispers. There are many Gospel Musicals that have been presented before many people where the power of the Lord has been experienced. We, as believers, will be standing around the Throne of God at sometime praising Him with His music like that described in the Book of Revelation.

> *Revelation 5:9-14, "And they sang a new song: 'You are worthy to take the scroll and to open its seals, because you were slain, and with your blood you purchased men for God from every tribe and language and people and nation. You have made them to be a kingdom and priests to serve our God, and they will reign on the earth.' Then I looked and heard the voice of many angels, numbering thousands upon thousands, and ten thousand times ten thousand. They encircled the throne and the living creatures and the elders. In a loud voice they sang: 'Worthy is the Lamb who was slain, to receive power and wealth and wisdom and strength and honor and glory and praise!' Then I heard every creature in heaven and on earth and under the earth and on the sea, and*

> *all that is in them, singing: 'To him who sits on the throne*
> *and to the Lamb be praise and honor and glory and power,*
> *for ever and ever!' The four living creatures said, 'Amen,' and*
> *the elders fell down and worshiped." NIV*

Can you imagine the beauty of many millions of people standing around the throne of God worshiping Him singing praises to God? We will one day give back some of the music that He has given to us to enjoy in true praise to the living God.

Whisper of God in Worship Services

Have you ever had an opportunity to stand in front of a church congregation to watch people's faces? Having been a Worship Leader for several years I find people to be extremely interesting to observe as they sing. Most people sing seeming as if they are in agony or just ate a dill pickle. Some people are smiling enjoying the music while worshiping the Lord. The music leader is trained to prepare spiritually before standing in front of a congregation so that God can work through him or her to become an effective worship prompter. When you are the leader or one of the praise team leaders, you must focus on the Lord Jesus within your heart. Watch the people and prompt them to worship with you. Part of the responsibility of a worship leader was to welcome the Lord to whisper His love to His people at the very moment they opened their hearts to Him.

There was a lady who seemed to be watching me very closely in a worship service. She did not smile, nor was she singing, but she was watching what was going on in the service. When the music portion of the service ended, we all sat down to listen to the sermon that followed. I was called forward at the end of the service to be available for the response time and suddenly this woman came right up to me asking me to lead her to the Lord. She told me that she was told within her heart that I would be the one to share the truth of the Gospel of Jesus Christ with her that morning. Her name was Candy, and what a blessing it was to be able to share Jesus with her that morning. She later became a member of the Sunday school class that I was teaching. Eventually asking her why she did not sing that morning and that she had been watching me? She said that she doesn't usually sing anyway, but she was fascinated at how I was smiling at her. She was looking for answers as to why she had not died yet, because she had survived breast cancer and a liver transplant. She knew that God must have a plan for her life. He does have a plan, and He still is working through her life today. She teaches the Word of God now as a teacher of a women's Bible study that is held in her home. This is the reason that you should watch people when you are given an opportunity to be a worship leader because the Pastor is not always the person that God works through to direct a person to Jesus Christ. He asks us to only be available while He whispers to a person's heart.

> *Psalms 89:1-4 "I will sing of the Lord's great love forever; with my mouth I will make your faithfulness known through all generations. I will declare that your love stands firm forever, that you established your faithfulness in heaven itself. You said, 'I have made a covenant with my chosen one, I have sworn to David my servant, 'I will establish your line forever and make your throne firm through all generations.''" NIV*

Jesus Christ is the promised one that came through the line of David. God has kept His promise to King David because he had a heart that heard the message from God that caused him to repent and to continue to worship the one true God.

David sings for God through the Psalms

King David had a heart for God's music. He played his harp to sooth King Saul, and he wrote music that he used to pray and worship God. Most of the Psalms were written from his heart, and this displayed the deep relationship that he had with God. There have been studies created from all the Psalms, but one of my favorites is Psalms 51. There has been music written for several of the Psalms today.

> *Psalms 51:10-11, "Create in me a pure heart, O God, and renew a steadfast spirit within me. Do not cast me from your presence or take your Holy Spirit from me." NIV*

I did not quote all of the scripture, but the message of David's heart prayed asking God to forgive him and to create in him a pure heart. I truly believe that this is the real reason that David was remembered to be the man after God's own heart. We all make mistakes and sin. When we want to be favored by God, we must follow the example this Psalm expresses. We should see our sin in the light of a perfect and loving God. A superficial "I am sorry" statement is not enough, but we must not punish ourselves unnecessarily either. David sang songs of joy once he knew that God had forgiven him. King David was a singer, and he continued to write many songs expressing his faith. Writers of music today express their faith and teach about the lessons they have learned from the Holy Spirit through music. Their stories through music may touch us because we have learned that same lesson.

"Mercy Saw Me" is an anointed song. This music piece has been used to prepare my heart for prayer in my private closet. The words to the music take me back before I was saved and remind me that it was because of mercy that I am saved and am righteous before an Almighty God. Mercy is another name for Jesus. Jesus saw what I could become and not what I was. I am thankful to the heart of Craig Nelson who wrote this music and who heard the whisper of God.

In II Chronicles 30-31 during his reign King Hezekiah chose to restore the Temple for worshiping God. He sent a message to all his people asking them to consecrate themselves once again to return to worshiping God. Some people mocked him, but those who did return to worshiping God in the Temple sang songs of praise making the offerings that were required at this time in history. The Lord heard their prayers and the songs of praise. The land returned to being prosperous once again. Let us turn our hearts back to the Lord in prayer and praising God with music, so that He will bless our land again.

God truly inhabits our praises through the power of music.

1. *Pray:*

Lord, thank you for music that draws us close to you. Thank you for allowing your Holy Spirit to whisper to us that which convicts us of sin, but lovingly guides us back to you when we stray. Music is a whisper to us from your heart to our heart. Help us to worship you from our heart through the gift of music.

2. *Reflection:*

Has God's music whispered a message to you? What has been your favorite kind of music? Are you willing to listen to music that you have not heard before?

CHAPTER 4

The Whisper of
Generations Past

S ometimes I have envisioned the faithful of generations past watching
our activity here as we serve the Lord. It seems like we have a
cheering group of souls saying to us to keep faithful to the Lord!
The Bible is full of servants who served the Lord and sometimes failed
Him. The Bible does say that there is a cloud of witnesses that surround
us. Who is this crowd?

> *Hebrews 12:1-3, "Therefore, since we are surrounded by such*
> *a great cloud of witnesses, let us throw off everything that*
> *hinders and the sin that so easily entangles, and let us run*
> *with perseverance the race marked out for us. Let us fix our*
> *eyes on Jesus, the author and perfecter of our faith, who for the*
> *joy set before him endured the cross, scorning its shame, and*
> *sat down at the right hand of the throne of God. Consider*
> *him who endured such opposition from sinful men, so that*
> *you will not grow weary and lose heart." NIV*

We should be thankful to those who wrote their stories. Who were
the faithful that broke the barrier to proclaim Jesus Christ as the Savior?

Whether they are biologically related or not we have their stories that encourage our faith. People came to North America under great stress and persecution to start fresh with their families. Many left loved ones behind and lost loved ones in their journey.

The book of Hebrews in the 11th chapter credits men and women for their faith and their relationships with God. They believed God! God made promises and gave them wisdom. He gave them directions, and some names were mentioned. There were thousands of followers whose names were never mentioned, but who still received their inheritance as promised in the Bible. The inheritance came through Jesus Christ. This was the gift of eternal life and being in the presence of a Holy God.

When we believe in the power of the GRACE that Jesus Christ offers, we can live an abundant life here and now in our physical life. We never out give what God the Father has given to the people of faith.

When we begin to understand the magnitude of His love, through His sacrifice, He has provided for the believer, we desire to do some little thing that would please Him. His love for us will motivate us to want what He wants and to listen for the whisper of His plan. Our nation was originally built on Christian principles, but not everyone who came to the new world was a believer.

The novel *Roots* by Alex Haley awakened our emotions to the cruelty of slavery, but we came to admire those that fought to survive! We are encouraged by the accomplishments of those who pushed forward to change our nation for the better. The book was made into a "mini-series" and all nationalities were emotionally stirred. The desire for people to get to know their past was nurtured in the hearts of many people, including people of faith. The evil was evident, but humanity has been mistreating each other for centuries. The choice is for each person to become a better person, caring for his fellowman. We can choose to be bitter and allow the cruelty to continue, but this would be a sad decision. Let us strive to make our world around us a better place to live!

Our modern day computer allows people to network with other people who have searched past generations. The families have been found and have begun to understand more about where they have come from and the family belief systems. There is a deeper understanding as to where families migrated from and why they settled where they did. The families were striving to find a better life. It seems that several people wandered like lost sheep while some people were driven to migrate because their faith was motivated by the Holy Spirit of God to guide them. Was the United States truly a country that was founded on Christian belief and freedom? There were people that were persecuted all over the world for their desire to follow the faith they had in Jesus Christ!

We move around today more often than our ancestors did due to the availability of transportation that is available to us. What is God's Holy Spirit doing in our world to reveal His truth of who He is and His powerful love? The generations past, who have been believers, is one-way God will whisper to our hearts. God does work through people to do His divine work. He has given wisdom to His people to bring a gentle light to encourage humanity today.

The Bible discourages people to talk about endless genealogies because people should not be the focus of worship. The reason for writing this chapter is to share the light of the message of their faith in Jesus Christ. The generations past in my family have inspired me to be a woman of faith and to listen for their messages to me. What were their messages? What did they do to glorify God? How did they respond to God's love? What motivated them to serve the Lord? What driving force made them choose the activity they accomplished? How did they encourage others in their faith? I am telling you right now that they reflected a sinful nature, too. Some of their same weaknesses are visible in my life. The GRACE of Jesus Christ was profoundly evident through their lives when they humbled themselves to be sensitive to the guidance of the Holy Spirit.

We cannot say to ourselves, "because my father was a preacher" then I am good with God! Let us read a scripture together that clarifies this truth that came from the teaching of Jesus Christ. He makes it clear that it is not who we are related to that makes us righteous before a Holy God.

> *John 8:39-48, They answered and said to Him, "Abraham is our father." Jesus said to them, "If you were Abraham's children, you would do the works of Abraham. But now you seek to kill Me, a Man who has told you the truth which I heard from God. Abraham did not do this. You do the deeds of your father. "Then they said to Him, "We were not born of*

*fornication; we have one Father — God." Jesus said to them,
"If God were your Father, you would love Me, for I proceeded
forth and came from God; nor have I come of Myself, but He
sent Me. Why do you not understand My speech? Because you
are not able to listen to My word. You are of your father the
devil, and the desires of your father you want to do. He was
a murderer from the beginning, and does not stand in the
truth, because there is no truth in him. When he speaks a lie,
he speaks from his own resources, for he is a liar and the father
of it. But because I tell the truth, you do not believe Me.
Which of you convicts Me of sin? And if I tell the truth, why
do you not believe Me? He who is of God hears God's words;
therefore you do not hear, because you are not of God. NKJV*

The scripture is very clear and does not need to be explained. Abraham's story has been a blessing from generation to generation. Have you heard the whisper of Abraham's message? Have you heard the message from your grandmothers, mothers, grandfathers or fathers who have opened the path to encourage your faith in Jesus Christ?

Huguenot

I want to write a story about a Huguenot immigrant, but first I want to share their story of who they were and what they faced before coming to North America. This information came from the "**The National Huguenot Society**".

"The Huguenots were French Protestants most of whom eventually came to follow the teachings of John Calvin, and who, due to religious persecution, were forced to flee France to other countries in the sixteenth and seventeenth centuries. Some remained, practicing their faith in secret. The Protestant Reformation began by Martin Luther in Germany about 1517, spread rapidly in France, especially among those having grievances against the established order of government. As Protestantism grew and developed in France it generally abandoned the Lutheran form, and took the shape of Calvinism. The new "Reformed religion" practiced by many members of the French nobility and social middle-class, based on a belief in salvation through individual faith without the need for the intercession of a church hierarchy and on the belief in an individual's right to interpret scriptures for themselves, placed these French Protestants in direct theological conflict with both the Catholic Church and the King of France in the theocratic system which prevailed at that time. Followers of this new Protestantism were soon accused of heresy against the Catholic government and the established religion of France, and a General Edict urging extermination of these heretics (Huguenots) was issued in 1536. Nevertheless, Protestantism continued to spread and grow, and about 1555 the first Huguenot church was founded in a home in Paris based upon the teachings of John Calvin. The number and influence of the French Reformers (Huguenots) continued to increase after this event, leading to an escalation in hostility and conflict between the Catholic Church/State and the Huguenots. Finally, in 1562, some 1200 Huguenots were slain at Vassey, France, thus igniting the French Wars of Religion, which would devastate France for the next thirty-five years."

Daniel DuVal (1675 –died after 1718) was a Chevalier of France, and his spouse Philadelphia Dubois were both from France. He was a Huguenot, and she was a nominal Catholic. Her uncle, Guillaume Dubois, was a French cardinal and statesman who aided them to elope in England. They married and boarded a ship. After the revocation of the "Edict of Nantes" he became a refugee to England and sailed on board the ship, *Le Nasseau,* under Captain Tragian on Dec 8, 1700 landing in the York River March 3, 1701. They settled in Gloucester County, Virginia. There is a church called Ware Parish Church in Gloucester County Virginia where Daniel DuVal and his family were members. It is thought that Daniel helped build this structure. (This information came from personal research within my family structure.)

This family came to the United States so they could worship God with freedom from the persecution that was happening in France. Through the family line one member, William DuVal, was named the first United States Governor of the new Florida Territory.

Another member of the family, Claiborne Lawson DuVal (1788-1834) was ordained a Methodist Episcopal minister in 1816. After several years as a circuit rider, he founded and pastored Antioch M.E. Church about 1820 near Morganfield, making him the first Methodist pastor in that county.

This was just a short description of one family that contributed to making the United States a better place to live. They worshiped freely and spoke to their children about the sacrifices they chose to make to leave their families behind in France for freedom to express their faith. I truly believe that God blessed them. Two of Daniel DuVal's sons fought in the Revolutionary War, Daniel DuVal II and Joseph DuVal. Daniel DuVal II was a Lt Colonel, and Joseph was killed as a public servant. This line came through my paternal grandmother, Martha Ellen Holman, who was a believer in Jesus Christ. Her great grandmother was Elizabeth DuVal who married Henry Bowles Holman.

Do you think for a moment that this family would ask people to honor them? What would be the message that was whispered to them that would give us strength to make changes in our life? Would God ever ask us to move away from our families and join Him in an adventure that would help us touch other people's lives? How much more would you grow to depend on a Holy Father in heaven? Would you trust His plan? I believe our nation was founded on the faith of people like this family.

You are asking, what does this family mean to me? This family line is part of my family line. Daniel DuVal was my sixth generation grandfather. I am humbled that the Holy Spirit revealed this blessing to me. I hope this encourages you to search for the message of your "roots".

Abraham was told by God to leave his country and to go to the land where He would show Him. Let us read the scripture together. Abraham's obedience to the whisper of God came with promises.

> *Genesis 12:1-3, "The Lord had said to Abram, 'Leave your country, your people and your father's household and go to the land I will show you. I will make you into a great nation and I will bless you; I will make your name great, and you will be a blessing. I will bless those who bless you, and whoever curses you I will curse; and all peoples on earth will be blessed through you.'" NIV*

Sater Baptist Church in Maryland

Inscription: On land granted by the Fifth Lord Baltimore, Henry Sater, gentleman planter, founded this first church of Baptists in Maryland. To the congregation he deeded a plot and chapel "forever to the end of the world." This message is located in front of the church that still stands.

In 1742, Henry Sater, deeded a plot of land for people to come and worship the Savior, Jesus Christ. He migrated from England at the age of nineteen. He wanted the freedom to worship God and to own his own land. Our family has stated that he was considered a black Dutch, which means something for different time periods. The most common statement is that these people were from Spanish and Dutch decent reflecting dark, or black hair, and olive colored skin. One of the examples used was "Elvis Presley". Some documents say that they came from Jewish descendents that migrated to the Netherlands and then into England. My mother's name was Bernice Sater, and she did have black hair and olive skin. Henry Sater is another sixth generation grandfather. I have done some research, and the Sater name was changed from Satyr, which is Jewish. This confirms that the black Dutch was from Jewish and Dutch decent in my family. It seems that the Holy Spirit keeps opening the doors to information. This is just to remind me that God already knows everything and that His wisdom is ready to be given when it is His timing. (Note: There is further information in the last chapter of this book.)

Here is an article written by W. Loyd Allan from "You are a great People";

In 1709, Henry Sater sailed from England, landed somewhere on the Virginia shores and soon made his way up the Chesapeake Bay into northern parts of the province of Maryland. He bore with him the Baptist faith of his homeland, the seed of Maryland's Baptist future. He was nineteen.

When he came over from England, he purchased a tract of land on what was then known as "Chestnut Ridge," about nine miles northwest of "Baltimore town." Sater cultivated tobacco and was a slave owner. His plantation profited from his slaves' unpaid labor.

His first recorded land grant was fifty acres obtained seven years after he sailed, and it was transferred with a purchase price of 120 pounds of tobacco in accord with a proprietary agreement put forward in 1684. Sater acquired in excess of a thousand acres by similar means over the next twelve years, each time paying in the currency of the day: tobacco. He erected a meetinghouse and graveyard, which was carved out of his tobacco plantation. Among the travelers from eastern Pennsylvania, Maryland and Virginia, there was found, occasionally, a Baptist minister, and Mr. Sater always invited him to his "plantation" to preach at his dwelling. In 1742 Sater deeded the meeting house, which was on his own land, for the church. July 10, 1742, the Baptist way took permanent root in Maryland soil. For more than three decades Sater had cultivated tobacco and Baptist principles in and around the primeval forests of Chestnut Ridge, Maryland. In Sater's fifty-third year, he saw the fruit of his labor ripen into Maryland's first Baptist church as fifty-seven persons signed a "solemn league and covenant," forming the Chestnut Ridge General Baptist congregation (later called Saters). (See covenant below.) Mr. Sater bore an excellent character. His assistance in building the place of worship and his gifts of land to the ministry are mentioned as peculiar marks of his liberality. He was instrumental in constituting the earliest Baptist church in the colony.

The covenant, under which this church was organized, is a unique politico-ecclesiastical document.

> *"We, the humble professors of the Gospel of Christ, baptized upon a declaration of faith and repentance, believing the doctrine of general redemption (or free grace of God to all mankind), do hereby, seriously heartily and solemnly, in the presence of the Searcher of all hearts, and before the world, covenant, agree, bind, arid settle ourselves into a church, to hold, abide by, and contend for the faith once delivered to the saints, owned by the best reformed churches in England, Scotland, and elsewhere, especially as published and maintained in the forms and confessions of the Baptists in England and Scotland, except in infant baptism, modes of church government, the doctrine of absolute reprobation, and some ceremonies. We do also bind ourselves hereby to defend and live up the protestant religion, and abhor and oppose the*

whore of Rome, pope and popery, with all her anti-Christian ways. We do also engage, with our lives and fortunes, to defend the crown and dignity of our gracious sovereign, King George, to him and his issue for ever; and to obey all his laws, humbly submitting ourselves to all in authority under him, and giving custom to whom custom, honor to whom honor, tribute to whom tribute is due. We do further declare that we are not against taking oaths, nor using arms in defense of our king and country, when legally called thereto; and that we do approve and will obey the laws of this Province. And further, we do bind ourselves to follow the patterns of our brethren in England to maintain order, government, and discipline in our church, especially that excellent directory of Rev. Francis Stanley, entitled 'The Gospel Honor and Church Ornament', dedicated to the churches in the counties of Lincoln, Nottingham, and Cambridge. We also engage that all persons, upon joining our society, shall yield consent to and subscribe this our solemn league and covenant. Subscribed by us whose names are underwritten, this 10th day of July, 1742."

Sater was born in 1689 in England. Sater worked for decades before starting a family. He married in 1730, his fortieth year, and soon thereafter became a childless widower. In 1740 he married Dorcas Towson, the daughter of blacksmith and original Chestnut Ridge church trustee William Towson. They had four sons and two daughters. When Sater made his last will and testament in 1753, he had significant property to bequeath to his four sons, but could not write his own name; he called as witness to the will a member of the Quakers. Henry Sater died in May of 1754.

Henry Sater is the great-great-great grandfather of Annie Armstrong."

Let us look at another scripture and the setting is just before Jesus left the disciples after He was crucified and had risen from the dead. He was teaching them to go forth and share the truth of who He was and what power God the Father had given Him. He promised that He would be with believers forever.

Mathew 28:18-20, Then Jesus came to them and said, "All authority in heaven and on earth has been given to me. Therefore go and make disciples of all nations, baptizing them in the name of the Father and of the Son and of the Holy Spirit, and teaching them to obey everything I have commanded you. And surely I am with you always, to the very end of the age." NIV

Who is Annie Armstrong?

Annie Armstrong never married, but gave her life to prayer and writing. She wrote over 18,000 letters to believers in the known world, at that time, encouraging people to financially support foreign missionaries who were starving overseas while they served the Lord. Her greatest concern was for Lottie Moon, a missionary in China. She humbly began her service at the age of nineteen when she first became a believer and taught children about Jesus. She strived to get written documents in the hands of believers so that they could grow under the grace of Jesus and to understand the power of the word. Women had a difficult time getting recognized and heard at the time she lived, but she was proactive in the attempt to support the mission of Jesus Christ. There have been books and articles written about her over the years, so I have become acquainted with my caring and loving cousin. She was a person who honored the message of Jesus Christ and desired no personal attention. In fact, in the most current book written about her life she was not pleased that the Southern Baptist Denomination would use her name to promote mission's giving for home missionaries. She finally agreed to the use of her name just prior to her death. She was a humble servant who desired that the Lord Jesus Christ be glorified. Her message to me was to minister, in the power of the Holy Spirit, and encourage women in their faith.

The Whisper from Generation to Generation

There has been interest centered in the past today by television shows like "Who Do You Think You Are" and "Finding Your Roots". They focus on the famous or well-known people of today, but what about people not known? Just like the book of Hebrews, not all people are known by name, but only those people who have extended stories of faith have been told. I enjoy hearing family stories of faith because our biological families do have an influence on what we are interested in life. Our passions are motivated by something that we sometimes do not understand. I had no desire to write and could not write very well, so what motivated me?

I started the journey to find out who I was first by finding my great-grandfather, Rev Braxton McCord Roberts (1810-1883). I have written about him in the first two books that have been published, so I will not go into details. I began my search because I did not know my heritage or my grandparents. I have passions that are similar in the hearts of my family, whom I never knew personally. My faith in Jesus Christ deepened for the desire to read God's Word and pray for others. God has had His touch in the lives of people from generation to generation. We are all seeds of Abraham due to our faith in a Holy God that gave freedom and grace to people that trust in Jesus Christ. There is a whisper that comes through in the Bible through families in the past that have reached our hearts today. My prayer is that we keep the message of salvation for future generations to know and understand. God instructed families to tell their children about what God had for them.

There was an article that was written called "What happened to Judah?" by Gladys Taylor. She explains how the migration of the tribe of Judah traveled until the journey ended in Britain. Joseph of Arimathea, mentioned in the Bible as the one that donated his tomb to bury Jesus Christ, after His crucifixion, was influential in sharing the message of Jesus Christ in Britain. It said that Jesus Christ was his great nephew and possible uncle to Mary. Mary was the mother of Jesus. It was written that when Joseph of Arimathea came to Britain, his children married into the Silurian house. Joseph is mentioned in several ancient Welch genealogies and is named in the triad of "Three Saintly Lineages of the Island of Britain". You can "google" the entire article to read and review. One interesting statement that I focused on was *So we see the purpose of God being fulfilled.*

Psalms 145:10-13, "All you have made will praise you, O Lord; your saints will extol you. They will tell of the glory of your kingdom and speak of your might, so that all men may know of your mighty acts and the glorious splendor of your kingdom. Your kingdom is an everlasting kingdom, and your dominion endures through all generations." NIV

There was another story passed down through my family about a man named Rev. Samuel S Headlee. He was a residing elder of the Springfield District for the M.E. Church South. He was attempting to reorganize the church and was shot down by villains who were opposed to his preaching. This man served the Lord and was killed attempting to bring the Gospel to the community where he was living. He knew the danger he was facing, but moved forward in the power of the Holy Spirit. His death motivated people to fight for the truth of the Gospel of Jesus Christ. This information came from an article written from "Martyrdom in Missouri, Volume II, p.428) There is more information written in the book than what I have personally written. He was willing to give his life for the truth of God's Word.

1. *Pray:*

   Help me Lord to listen to the whispers from my past generations and use my family history to assist me to walk closer with you. If my family did not have a faith history, then let it begin with me. Amen

2. *Reflection*

   How would you benefit by exploring the origin of your family roots? Listen for God's whisper as you discover your personal heritage.

CHAPTER 5

The Whisper Through Victorious Testimonies

Romans 8:31-39, What then shall we say to these things? If God is for us, who can be against us? He who did not spare His own Son, but delivered Him up for us all, how shall He not with Him also freely give us all things? Who shall bring a charge against God's elect? It is God who justifies. Who is he who condemns? It is Christ who died, and furthermore is also risen, who is even at the right hand of God, who also makes intercession for us. Who shall separate us from the love of Christ? Shall tribulation, or distress, or persecution, or famine, or nakedness, or peril, or sword? As it is written:

"For Your sake we are killed all day long;
We are accounted as sheep for the slaughter."

Yet in all these things we are more than conquerors through Him who loved us. For I am persuaded that neither death nor life, nor angels nor principalities nor powers, nor things present nor things to come, nor height nor depth, nor any

other created thing, shall be able to separate us from the love
of God which is in Christ Jesus our Lord. NKJV

We all face difficulties through our lifetime and sometimes there is no warning. The testimonies that will be shared in this chapter are true. The whisper of God's powerful love is revealed through the victory of these lives that have been willing to tell their testimonies. I have seen the glow on their faces as they talked to me regarding their past experiences and what God is doing in their lives today.

Story of Abuse

This is the testimony of a woman by the name of Cindy. She is now married with 5 children. She and her husband are delightful people, in the Lord, but it was not always this way in her life. She was willing to share her testimony, so that the Lord would be glorified.

She grew up as a twin and had several siblings. Her story started by sharing her earliest memory, which when was 9 years old. She and her siblings had been beaten severely where they were all left with bruises and open wounds to their bodies and the faces. All the children were in their underwear waiting for their father to go to bed. They remained quiet as they walked out into the backyard of their house. They decided that they would lift the youngest of the children over the stone fence into the alley so that he could run to a neighbor's to get help for all of them. He landed on top of a police car hood instead. Startled, the policeman jumped out of the patrol car asking the young boy questions. He noticed the open wounds, the bruises and the lack of clothing. The child told him that he needed help for his other brothers and sisters, too. It was not very long when the police entered the home to get the other children to remove them from this house.

Cindy said that all the children were beaten almost every night before going to bed. She remembers most of her beatings were facial and other areas that could be hidden with clothes. The abuse did not end in her biological family, but it was the beginning.

Cindy and her siblings were placed into the Foster Care Program of the state where she was living. She moved from house to house being abused by most of the foster parents and becoming angry, as she grew older. She ran away from several foster homes choosing to live on the street, along with other teenagers. She stated that her anger is what kept her alive. She and her friends had to steal to survive. Cindy continued to share that when she was about 14 years old she remembers digging through garbage cans to find food to eat. She stated that she became quite experienced in where to look, what time and what places would be the safest places to find the food. As she continued to share I became very shocked at the conditions in which she lived. She said it was better to live on the street than in some of the foster homes in which she was placed where they would take the money for themselves and not provide her with the clothes and food she needed.

She was angry, rude and somewhat abusive with her mouth. She stated that there was a time she sat alone thinking about possibly ending her life, but then she said that her father would have won. She could not let that happen! She kept repeating that her anger kept her alive.

Cindy was eventually placed in a home for disturbed teenagers. Most of the staff considered her a lost cause that could not be changed from her angry state of mind. In walked a lady by the name of Betty to speak to her, and this woman was different. Cindy threatened her with Betty saying, "that will be alright with me". She was calm, at peace and unwavering in her kindness to Cindy. Cindy watched her for weeks wondering why Betty was the way she was in the personality that she expressed. Betty never treated Cindy in any other way but by pure kindness and love. Betty wanted to take Cindy home with her, so she did. Betty saw in Cindy a young lady who needed to be accepted, loved and cared for like she had never experienced before. Betty saw a beautiful young lady and began to share this with Cindy. Cindy began to slowly trust Betty and responded to her unconditional love for her in her new home. Betty and her husband adopted Cindy when she was 16 years old. Cindy now had a real, nurturing and loving home. Betty began to share the love of Jesus Christ with her when she knew that Cindy's heart was ready to receive this truth. Betty's transformed life through the power of faith revealed the love and acceptance that Jesus has for us when we repent of our sins.

Betty did not stop there, but she asked her son, Mark, to assist in tutoring Cindy in her studies, so that she could catch up with her schoolwork. Mark had already left home living out on his own. He agreed to assist his mother as she asked him to do. A romance began to develop between Cindy and Mark. Mark never took advantage of Cindy and this was the reason she began to really like him. She had already been touched abusively too many times to allow any man to get too close. Cindy accepted Jesus Christ as her Savior and slowly was being transformed by the power of faith that was being revealed to her by the Holy Spirit. The fullness of God's love within her allowed her to fall in love with Mark.

Mark and Cindy got married, growing in their faith together, and starting a family of their own. Betty is her mother and mother-in-law. Mark and Cindy have five children. There are three girls and two boys. They are all children of faith in the Lord Jesus Christ. Cindy has confessed that when her children were small she struggled with sparks of anger, but Mark was always there to gently assist her through these difficult times. He understood her past abusive experience. She said that he has truly been the power of Christ in their home.

Cindy is my friend; she and Mark support our ministry and walk along side of us to share the truth of God's love to people who are less fortunate in life's journey. She is out spoken still, but for all the right reasons now. Cindy is not ashamed of the Gospel of Jesus Christ.

The whisper of God's love was expressed through a woman of faith showed Cindy the way the Holy Spirit sees all sinners. God expresses Himself through faithful believers who have grown to have a close relationship with the Savior, Jesus Christ.

> *Romans 10:14-15, "How, then, can they call on the one they have not believed in? And how can they believe in the one of whom they have not heard? And how can they hear without someone preaching to them? And how can they preach unless they are sent? As it is written, 'How beautiful are the feet of those who bring good news!'" NIV*

An Unexpected Tragedy

This next story is about a lady by the name of Tillie. I first met this woman at our church one evening when she was visiting her family in

Oklahoma. She is retired and living in Florida as I write this part of her story that she has shared with me and with others in the past.

Tillie grew up in Oklahoma as a farm girl being the 5th born of 7 children. She stated that they were poor financially, but she never knew it. She remembers her parents praying every night for every child in the house by name. She knew she was blessed by living in a family who loved and served the Lord. Her mother and father lived their faith as a witness to all the children.

When she graduated from high school, she left home to go to nursing school. Her educational training took her three years to complete. Then she decided that she wanted to go a St. Paul Bible College, so she moved away to Minnesota. She was three weeks late during the first semester of being there. She had to finish nursing school. She became the school nurse, which paid for her room and board, tuition and the classes at the school. She was only there one week when she was called to care for a student who had the flu. There, during her first semester, she met her future husband, Bob, who was also a student. They met when a flu outbreak happened at the school. They were both asked to assist with the sick students by administering the needed medications. Tillie was a Registered Nurse and needed to provide the medication to the young men, so Bob was asked to go with her to their dorms. They became acquainted and began dating after the first of the New Year. They were married on August 22, 1958.

Bob's home state was Florida, so they moved to Florida where they started their family. There were three girls and one boy born to this couple over the next several years. Bob became a City Police Officer in Daytona Beach, Florida, and he was there two years. Then he became a Florida State Trooper working for the state for eight years. Tillie said that being a police officer's wife could be difficult from time to time, so during one of these difficult times her spiritual walk with God became non-existent. Then her husband was with the Navy Intelligence in 1969 through 1972. The name changed to "Defense Investigative Service" in 1972. They finally moved to Hollywood, Florida where they lived from 1985 to 1992.

Tillie prayed for her husband daily, placing his name where it may apply and hers, at the same time through Ephesians 3:14- 21 almost every day. She began to be changed by the power of these scriptures being read every day. She began to insert her children's names, missionaries, friends, other family members and her Pastor's name.

> *Ephesians 3:14-21, "For this reason I kneel before the Father, from whom his whole family in heaven and on earth derives its name. I pray that out of his glorious riches he may strengthen you with power through his Spirit in your inner being, so that Christ may dwell in your hearts through faith. And I pray that you, being rooted and established in love, may have power, together with all the saints, to grasp how wide and long and high and deep is the love of Christ, and to know this love that surpasses knowledge — that you may be filled to the measure of all the fullness of God. Now to him who is able to do immeasurably more than all we ask or imagine, according to his power that is at work within us, to him be glory in the church and in Christ Jesus throughout all generations, for ever and ever! Amen." NIV*

Tillie said that another scripture she would pray along with her own personal praise prayers was Colossians 1: 9-14.

Tillie wrote to me in a letter that she started using scriptures to pray when she and Bob went going through some of their personal trials. She did not want to pray out of anger and the hurt that she had in her heart at this time. She placed him on the Altar of God. She said the room would be full of the Sweet Aroma of the Holy Spirit. She continues by saying that it was wonderful and sometimes she would tell the Lord to send her more pain so she could experience that same fulfillment in her relationship with the Him.

Bob committed himself to the Lord again. In their new faith this couple would experience another tragedy. Their oldest daughter, married with two children, died suddenly from severe heart problems. She had grown up experiencing heart murmurs, but it was not an issue as she grew older, or so everyone thought. This tragedy brought Bob and Tillie closer to each other and to the Lord. The peace was there due to the knowledge that their daughter had placed her faith in Jesus Christ as Savior and Lord.

Tillie stated that she received a call from her family some time later in Oklahoma telling her that her mother had had several mini strokes that had left her weak. This left her unable to care for herself. Bob stated he could get a job transfer from where they were living in Florida to Oklahoma if she wanted to go to care for her mother. I believe that she stated that her mother was alone at this time and her father had passed away a few years back. Bob and Tillie had experienced a renewed married life through the power of faith for 8 years before moving back to Oklahoma in December in 1992.

Bob was transferred to working in the Federal Building in downtown Oklahoma City, Oklahoma. The office where he worked was just above the parking garage in the Federal Building. Tillie's mother passed on March 31, 1993, but the couple stayed living and working in Oklahoma. Tillie was hired by Aetna Insurance to gather information for patient's entering the hospital for different reasons. She would spend most of her time on the telephone approving or disapproving medical procedures that were being requested by physician's and/or hospitals.

The morning of April 19, 1995 Tillie and Bob got up to get ready for their jobs. She walked Bob to the door, gave him a big kiss and told that she really loved him. She went into the kitchen to prepare her lunch waiting for him to get in the car in. She remembers giving Bob an extra long hug and telling him how much she loved him. He returned the words back to her then he got in his car to go on to work. She stood on the porch waving good-bye as he drove away.

On April 19, 1995, at 9:02 a.m., an explosion ripped through the Alfred P Murrah Federal Building in Oklahoma City. Tillie was sitting at her desk answering telephone calls seemingly the only one on the telephone. There was a big explosion, but no one knew where this was coming from until someone turned on the television they had in the office. It was the Federal Building where her husband was employed. The office where Tillie worked was about 12 miles from downtown Oklahoma City.

Tillie remembers someone asking her to get off the telephone and that they would cover for her for a while. She was asked to go into the employee conference room when she was told that the Federal Building had been bombed. She was told that she could leave, and she chose to go home and wait. There was no answer from anyone regarding the whereabouts of her husband until the next day. By then her three children were with her at her home. The police called to ask if Bob had any dental records they could have, so the family went to the dentist where Bob had just had some work done. They took the records to where they were instructed to go and left the records. A few hours later the telephone rang to tell the family that Bob was confirmed as being among the dead.

Tillie and the rest of the family were in grief. The scriptures that Tillie prayed in the past for Bob remained in her heart on this tragic day. The Power of Faith is what sustained this family through this unexpected disaster. The Aroma of the Holy Spirit is what gave them all peace that only comes from a God that loved them. The whisper of God's love gave them peace.

The blast killed 168 people – 19 of them children – and injured hundreds as quoted by the News Media in Oklahoma City.

The Bible is full of stories of unexpected disasters like the story of Job. He was a man of great faith, but he began to lose his children, his livestock, his servants and his health began to suffer. The only living family member left was his wife, who in time, asked Job to curse God and die. Job had two well-meaning friends who came to counsel him about the sins that he may have committed. Why else would a man suffer so much loss? When you read the beginning of the book of Job you witness a conversation between Satan and God the Father. (Job 1:6-12) As you read on through the book of Job, Satan did his best, but Job never cursed God, because of the purity of power his faith he had in God. God, at the end of the book blessed Job more than he had ever been blessed before all the disasters had taken place. (Job 42:12-17)

Let us go back to Tillie and her life. The power of faith has sustained her and this has blessing her life today. She lives in Florida again where most of her children and friends live witnessing for Jesus Christ. She shares her story to encourage others that nothing can separate us from the love of Jesus Christ. The sweet aroma of the Holy Spirit fills her life through the prayers she continues to pray for herself and other people. She has the joy of the Lord that radiates in and through her life. She is living a life of victory due to the power of faith she has in Jesus Christ. She is busy in her church, caring for those who are sick, providing meals and taking time to call those who are lonely. She is an encouragement to her family and to those who have gotten to know her story and who she has become in Christ today. Tillie said one of her favorite scriptures she prays through is the entire Psalm 145. King David wrote this Psalm as he grew in power, passion and love for the Lord. He has been frequently been called a man after God's own heart. Oh, that we would all desire to grow in this way and to know the Lord as he did. The power that he had for the Lord blesses us today.

The niece to Tillie was a member of our church. Her name is Rhonda, and she is a young mother of four children. She has been touched by the power of faith that her aunt lived. Rhonda still grieves for her uncle as she shares her experience:

"I have always been touched by my aunt's faith. She, along with all of her brother's and sister's still had that kind of faith. My mother is one of her sister's.

One day while visiting with my aunt, just before the trials for McVeigh, we were speaking about the trials coming up and that she would be testifying. I said to her, "I don't know if I could testify, or not." She returned with a statement, "It won't be easy but I have forgiven him." Rhonda continues by saying, "I didn't respond, but I thought how could she forgive him after what he did? I was struggling with forgiving because of all the children that were lost that day. I was Christian at that time, but I was not walking by the power of faith like my aunt Tillie was doing. I understand now, because I know that God wants us to forgive. If we are to be Christ like, we have to follow his example completely. I have learned all this through my aunt's example of her love for Jesus and then for others.

Let me go back to April 19, 1995. I was working in the stock room at Wal-Mart. Someone walking by said that there had been a bomb exploded in down town Oklahoma City. My first thought was for my aunt Tillie, because she did not work very far from the downtown area. I figured that my uncle was fine. I knew that he worked for the Department of Defense and thought that he was working on the base. I called my Mom and asked her to call aunt Tillie to see if she was all right, because I had just heard that a bomb had gone off in Oklahoma City. She returned my phone a short time later stating that aunt Tillie was fine, but uncle Bob was missing. I was devastated. I went to management, and they allowed me to join the rest of my family to go be with aunt Tillie. We went down the same day and took pictures when the fence was within a block of the building. I will never forget the feeling I had of sadness, mourning and knowing that there had been a lot of death that day.

I have gone every year on the anniversary of the bombing and have always felt the same way until I was able to forgive. The building of the reflective pool and the all the chairs and walls have assisted in helping me to heal and forgive. The Lord has given me His peace and gently began to teach me what the power of faith can accomplish when healing needs to take place in a life that has surrendered to His love."

The families will always grieve over that day. There is a beautiful and humbling memorial now where the building used to stand. Marty, our son Dale and I walked through the Memorial in the fall of 2007. Marty stopped in front of every picture to pray for the families of those lost that day not knowing that in the future we would be acquainted with one of those families. People that belong to God are a touch of God's hand in this world where we all live.

I want to thank Tillie for sharing her story with me and now, as you have read, she has shared her story with you. Let us be encouraged to live in victory as she has chosen to live. The disturbances we may experience such as a traffic ticket, a rainstorm or the attitude of another person that we cannot control can be overlooked when we know that it could be worse. The world can be full of disappointments, but we have a Savior that walks with us if we surrender to His love and understanding. Our Savior will lift us up as we choose to get to know him through power of faith.

Romans 8:28-30, "And we know that in all things God works for the good of those who love him, who have been called according to his purpose. For those God foreknew he also predestined to be conformed to the likeness of his Son, that he might be the firstborn among many brothers. And those he predestined, he also called; those he called, he also justified; those he justified, he also glorified." NIV

Cancer Diagnosis

This is my testimony in hopes that Jesus would be glorified. I have been healthy all my life, but I found a lump in my right breast. I did not have health insurance and after making several phone calls no doctor's office would accept me as a patient. I was told to go to the emergency room. I knew this would be expensive. I told my husband, but he did not encourage me to go to a doctor because we did not have the money. I began to pray fervently, but I would not tell any of my believing Christian friends nor my family because it has always been hard for me to ask for prayers for myself. Every day that I felt the lump, I prayed.

Finally, I had a long conversation with my husband and I became insistent about going to see a doctor. Out of anger my husband stopped at a small town medical clinic. I walked in and they had only a Nurse Practitioner on staff. I made an appointment for the next day. I went in for the appointment, and he confirmed my worst fear and referred me to the closest hospital for a mammogram. The office charged only $5.00 for the visit. Two days later I got a mammogram and an ultrasound. The Radiologist confirmed that I had breast cancer. We scheduled a biopsy, which reconfirmed the diagnosis.

My husband and I were campground hosts and there was a knock at the door of our recreational vehicle. It was a pastor friend and his wife visiting the campground. They wanted to visit with us for a while. We told them the news that we just received. He told us that God was in control and that he had just survived liver cancer and the treatments. We prayed together and turned it over to the Lord. The day before my surgery this same pastor friend came back with a large church group camping near by where we were working. We were asked to come to visit while he shared a message with the group. When he closed his message, he shared my circumstances and thirty-three people laid their hands on me to pray.

Within three weeks I was having surgery at this same hospital with another pastor friend and a deacon who had driven over one hundred miles to be close with us in prayer and support. Our daughter called just before I went into surgery. There were hundreds of people praying for me, and I was at peace. After Two days in the hospital and then was sent home to recover from the surgery for the next six weeks. I was scheduled to see an

Oncologist who sent me to have additional tests to see if the cancer had spread. The follow up visit showed that they had gotten all the cancer, but I needed to go through chemotherapy. We agreed to have the treatment and this lasted for six months. We have been blessed with having the entire surgery and most of the treatments being covered by the Susan G Komen grant fund. The journey has brought me closer to the Lord. He is in control, and He whispered His blessings to me. It has been three years and I am still cancer free thanks to the prayers of many friends and family. Do not be afraid to include other believers in any recovery you may be facing.

Jeremiah 17:14, Heal me, O Lord, and I will be healed; save me and I will be saved, for you are the one I praise. NIV

What about Today's Victory for you?

You may have a story of victory that made a change in your life. It may have given you a different outlook in the way you look at life today. Has God whispered His love to you through this experience? Write your story down and allow God to whisper through your story to others.

1. *Pray:*
   Lord, may the glory of your presence and peace be whispered to those who have read these testimonies. May they find your strength in their circumstances they may be facing today.

1. *Reflection:*
   Have you won a victory today, in Christ? Have you told your testimony to someone?

CHAPTER 6

The Whisper of God's Plan

Human beings are creatures of choices, of habit, of opinions, of talent and everyone has a biological mother and a father. The human mind is amazing in that it is capable of learning from birth to adulthood. The family structure molds the growing child's thinking, both negative and positive. The environment has an influence on the personalities that develop. The people who live near an individual will either contradict or encourage certain attitudes. There are several factors in all of humanity that influence the future from day to day. People make choices on who they will associate with and who can influence their attitude and actions. Some people come from abusive homes, some from neglectful homes, some from financially challenged homes, some from financially wealthy homes and some from homes that teach the truth of Jesus Christ. Some people have grown knowing what they were going to do for the rest their lives. Maybe Dad and Mom owned a cattle farm, so the son continues the family tradition. Maybe Dad or Mom was a doctor, so the family tradition spurred a person to become involved in the medical field. Through the history of the European culture, the King's sons were the next to follow in ruling a kingdom. There are different teachings due to a numerous number of religions that are in our world today. The Bible is not always the choice of truth in a home. When does one decide what the truth is and how is the truth revealed to an individual? Are there people who will never understand the truth of God's plan? Are there people, who claim to be believers who don't understand God's Plan? Are there people that are predestined to believe? Let us search the scriptures together for how God whispered to humanity and how He revealed His whisper to the heart of a child, man or a woman. The choice of influence for this writing is the Bible, commonly know as the Word of God.

> *Proverbs 19:21, Many are the plans in a man's heart, but it is the Lord's purpose that prevails. NIV*

The Whisper to the Child

> *Ps 139:13-16, "For you created my inmost being; you knit me together in my mother's womb. I praise you because I am fearfully and wonderfully made; your works are wonderful, I know that full well. My frame was not hidden from you when I was made in the secret place. When I was woven together in the depths of the earth, your eyes saw my unformed body. All the days ordained for me were written in your book before one of them came to be." NIV*

A child is beautifully made by God and formed in the womb of a woman from two single cells to develop a human being within nine months. The creator has plans for this child before he or she is born. King David knew very well that he was fearfully and wonderfully made, so he praised the God that made heaven and earth. He knew that God was witnessing his growth every day as he developed in the secret plan. He knew that his days were numbered and that God was in control of those days. God watched as David slept. He knew when David awakened every day, when he sat with his family to have a meal, when he had arguments with his siblings and when he got his first knee scrape. When the day came for him to be born, God had a plan for David, and when he grew older, he worked as a shepherd boy tending his father's sheep. He was learning every day that he lived by working in the field about the God who loved him. He would, in the fullness of God's time, become king of Israel.

Do you suppose that maybe for every child that is born that God may have a plan? To know the heart of God and His plans you must be taught with the knowledge that there is a God from the early stages of childhood. Children are open to the truth because their minds and hearts are so fresh to learning. They seem to have an understanding that enlightens an adult's heart at times. Their minds are creative and full of imagination. When you share the truth that there is a God, that He watches over the child, that He loves the child and that He created that child to have a special purpose. God's desire is for that child to have a relationship with Him. The child listens and believes what you are sharing with him or her. The parent(s) who are believers teach hope, love and guidance to the child that leaves the heart of the child open to seek the divine plan that the Creator intended for him in the future. You may not have been raised this way, but there is hope for you now as you read these words. Start today to understand that you are special and wonderfully made, no matter what your age is now.

When the child begins to develop he learns to be disobedient. The child will test the parents to see how far he/she can go due to his curious nature. Their minds and hearts are watching a sinful world around them. If there is no spiritual guidance, then the child will learn to be like the world he lives in and that is the world of darkness. Discipline is important to direct an attitude that honors his mother and father.

> *Proverbs 22:6, "Train a child in the way he should go, and when he is old he will not turn from it." NIV*

My question to you is do you believe this scripture is right, Mom and Dad? Should parent(s) discipline a child? There is a fine line between discipline and child abuse. There have been some wise statements made through out my growing up that said "never discipline a child when you are angry", or "listen to why the child did what he or she did". Are there alterative ways to discipline other then spanking or striking a child? What about the motive of being loved and not wanting the child to be in danger in the future? This is why God gave us the commandments in the Bible, and it was to protect us. He commanded us to love the Lord, our God, with all of our hearts, all of our minds, and with all of our soul. We are to love our neighbors as we love ourselves. The child grows to have a positive self-image when he is taught to understand these truths. The heart of a child can understand more than we realize.

> *"Proverbs 20:11, Even a child is known by his actions, by whether his conduct is pure and right." NIV*

Jesus was healing the sick, teaching in the synagogues, walking from village to village teaching about the Kingdom of God and visiting tax collectors in their homes. As He became known the crowds grew around Him wanting to be healed and some people were just following the crowd in curiosity. The heart of God, through the voice of Jesus, whispered a powerful truth regarding children. We are to be like children and have an open, accepting, heart. What is your age? Does it matter?

> *Mark 10:13-16, People were bringing little children to Jesus to have him touch them, but the disciples rebuked them. When Jesus saw this, he was indignant. He said to them, "Let the little children come to me, and do not hinder them, for the kingdom of God belongs to such as these. I tell you the truth, anyone who will not receive the kingdom of God like a little child will never enter it." And he took the children in his arms, put his hands on them and blessed them. NIV*

The Whisper to the Teenager

When you experience a Youth Ministry you witness the differences in teenagers. The boys want to strut in front of the girls to reflect their manhood. The girls flirt and like to tease the boys. These activities are normal when you have a large group. We have stated that teenagers are too old to be a little child, but too young to be an adult yet. Their emotions are erratic with the ups and downs of wanting to be accepted among their piers. There is always going to be the shy one that does not speak and the loud one that gets everyone's attention. Teenagers are blessings, and yet they can be difficult. The blessings come when you ask the group to take charge of a worship service in a church. They begin to search the Scriptures for ideas, and they pray together, as believers. We have seen a teenager begin and grow in their faith in the Lord Jesus Christ during these times. The heart of a believing teenager can reveal the truth of Jesus Christ to his or her unbelieving parents more than anyone. The parent may visit the church to witness that his teenager is involved in a worship service. This author could tell you many stories that she has witnessed through the teenager that has richly blessed her, but she will only share one story.

The activity planned was a Halloween Party for the Youth Group. They were told to be careful regarding their costumes, but some of the boys decided it would be fun to be scary. The decorations were put up, a soda fountain was rented and games were planned. The party was to run for four hours, and there were about 30 youth attending. One of the youth was dressed like an old man and carried a cane. No one knew who he or she might be, so this person became a guessing game with the other youth. The person allowed other youth to look in his eyes, and then he or she would smack them with his cane. Then during the last hour we instructed the kids to sit in a circle on the floor. The lights were dimmed and a light was placed in the middle of the circle with a foil over the light. A cross image had been cut into the foil, and it was reflected on the ceiling in the room. My husband had a large ball of yarn and instructed the young people to tell something about themselves or share their favorite Scripture. They were to throw the yarn to another person who they wanted to speak next. By the end of the activities it looked like a spider web, but everyone was connected. Everyone held on to part of the yarn. The Holy Spirit took over and the teenagers were sharing their deepest faith experiences. Tears were flowing, and hearts were being touched. Then the yarn reached our old man. She was a guest brought by one of the youth that was a member and a foreign missionary's daughter. She shared how she came to terms regarding her faith in Jesus Christ when her family had been arrested for sharing Christ. They all were placed against a wall to be shot and then a disruption caused the gunmen to flee. There was a not a dry eye in that room that night. Would your heart have been changed? Many of these youth are now serving the Lord, as adults. One of them became a missionary doctor, another an engineer who is a powerful witness for the Lord and others have families teaching their children the message of Jesus Christ. The whisper of the Holy Spirit to the hearts of everyone in the room was a powerful reminder of God's love and plan.

2 Timothy 1:7, For God did not give us a spirit of timidity,
but a spirit of power, of love and of self-discipline. NIV

The Whisper to a Young Adult

Young adults are often attending college somewhere, and they are finally away from the discipline or watchful care of their parents. Some young adults join the military to see the world or because they cannot afford the high cost of college. Some young girls get married to start their adult lives, but that does not happen as often as it did many years ago. Many young adults start their careers after graduating college or get married to start their families. They may be doing both: starting a career and getting married. The life of a young adult becomes very busy in the world of his chosen career as he works. It seems that spiritual matters are put aside for a while as they seek the incomes that allow them to buy expensive material items such as cars, houses, furniture, boats and jewelry. They spend their hard earned money on expensive entertainment. They attend baseball games, football games, ballets, opera, Broadway Shows, etc. This is not all bad, but where is their relationship with God in these activities?

God allows the young adult to enjoy life, but the heart of a young adult heart will change when the Holy Spirit whispers his name. The young adult becomes the blessing to the mission of the church and to furthering God's Plan. Many young adults are responding to being obedient to the prompting of the Holy Spirit by attending Seminaries across the United Stated. Young adults are leaving their countries and coming to attend seminaries so that they teach their own people the truth of Jesus Christ. The hearts of these precious young adults are giving more then 10% of their talent, time and money to serving the Lord all over the world. When my husband and I were young, we surrendered to God's call and heard Him whisper our name. Jesus could say to you, "Come to me, become available where I can work through you to equip and teach men, women and children." The Holy Spirit's whispers will give you His wisdom to become pastors, ministers and teachers of God's Word. My pastor brother committed to serving the Lord when he was eighteen years old and continues today. He has been a pastor, a Director of Missions and an interim pastor for over fifty years. He has always been available to instruct, equip and encourage young men and women entering the ministry. In the Bible Peter encourages the young men to listen to older believers in Jesus Christ. What about you?

> *1 Peter 5:5-9, "Young men, in the same way be submissive to those who are older. All of you, clothe yourselves with humility toward one another, because, 'God opposes the proud but gives grace to the humble.' Humble yourselves, therefore, under God's mighty hand, that he may lift you up in due time. Cast all your anxiety on him because he cares for you. Be self-controlled and alert. Your enemy the devil prowls around like a roaring lion looking for someone to devour. Resist him, standing firm in the faith, because you know that your brothers throughout the world are undergoing the same kind of sufferings." NIV*

We became acquainted with the young couple while we are attending seminary in California. They were fairly new believers in Jesus Christ. They lived next door to us in an apartment complex that was provided by the seminary. The young man of the couple attended and graduated with my husband from Golden Gate Baptist Theological Seminary. They later moved on to Colorado to serve in three churches over several years. This young man was a strong evangelical Christian believer. They had several challenges in the churches that they served. The Holy Spirit of God eventually led them to Tennessee. This young couple became parents of a beautiful little girl, and she was a miracle. In Tennessee the young man became a teacher to teenage believers during the summer months (Youth On A Mission). He has led several mission trips to foreign countries to reach people for the gospel of Jesus Christ. The couple went to the Holy land and to Russia to serve the Lord because of the whispers heard from the Holy Spirit. This couple has continued to hear the whispers of God as they have traveled and trusted God for their financial support through other believers. We receive newsletters and e-mails from them consistently sharing the miracles of following God's plan in their life.

Jesus Christ was the most powerful young adult that changed our world! His public ministry began when He was thirty years old and ended physically when He was thirty-three years old. He was and is the pure Lamb of God. He surrendered His life to take our place for the penalty of our sin. He is the veil of righteousness that gives us the right to be the called the children of God by faith. Jesus Christ was God's plan and promise to those who would believe.

> *John 3:16-18, "For God so loved the world that he gave his one and only Son, that whoever believes in him shall not perish but have eternal life. For God did not send his Son into the world to condemn the world, but to save the world through him. Whoever believes in him is not condemned, but whoever does not believe stands condemned already because he has not believed in the name of God's one and only Son."*
> *NIV*

The Whisper to the Median Adult

What is a median adult? The most common choice is from 39 to 55 years old, but it can differ in opinion. This is the time when people are well into their careers and are looking forward to possible retirement. Their children are almost grown or may even have left the nest. Some couples today may not have chosen to have children, or they may have started their families in their thirties. People make choices that are different in the 21st Century than those of generations past. This age group seems to make more diplomatic or well thought out decisions than any other time in their life. The choices they make can still be wrong decisions that are followed with heartache, grief and loss. We become sensitive in an attempt not to make those same decisions after an experience that has left us feeling out of control. There is still sin in everyone's life. We still need to humble our heart by asking for forgiveness from a Holy God. This needs to take place on a daily basis.

We knew a couple who started to attend the church where my husband was the pastor after their twin boys asked their father why they had to go to church if he didn't. Their entire family eventually accepted the Lord as their Savior. Their family, that included their elderly parents, were soon baptized. This family of five grew to become very active in the church. The wife taught the children's Bible class, and the husband began to teach the young adult class. The husband was vocationally working at the local landfill and working the family farm. The wife was a stay at home mom. When my husband resigned this new church, the congregation eventually asked this farmer to become their new pastor. He resigned the landfill job to serve the Lord full time. He is still their pastor and continues to work the family farm. The Lord touched the hearts of this couple when they were in their forties. They listened to the whispers of God and are still being sensitive to God's plan and will. Another couple, in that same church, is the pastor of another local church in the area. He had been the local furor in the Cheyenne, WYO area. His wife had taught the youth class. When the whisper of God is prompted in a believer's heart, it will change the direction that you have chosen. You will never be the same.

The joy of reaching this age, when you have followed the Lord's plan, is that He will continue to whisper to your hearts. He may alert you to new areas that you may not have thought of earlier in your walk with Him. Some of you may finally surrender to the ministry that the Holy Spirit was preparing your hearts to do a long time ago. He had to build your character for the assignment. Humility, wisdom and knowledge will come with time and a price. There was a thought that came to my heart one time, during prayer, when I thought I was too old for a certain ministry. The whisper came " And how old do you think I am?" This was a whisper from God! Well, ladies and gentlemen, we are never too old to follow the ministry that God has laid out for us to do. Have you heard the whisper of God to go in His name?

Matthew 10:27, "What I tell you in the dark, speak in the daylight; what is whispered in your ear, proclaim from the roofs." NIV

The Whisper to the Senior Adult

The most amazing senior adults in the Bible were Abraham and Sarai. As a young married couple they attempted to have children. When they got older, they still continued to try to have children. The custom at the time that they were living in was to have a son to carry on the family traditions of faith. When Sarai decided that she was too old to conceive, she offered her handmaiden Hagar to Abraham to give him the son that he so desired. Abraham agreed to Sarah's prompting and Hagar became pregnant with Ishmael, Abraham's first son. Later on in their lives Angels came to visit with the message for Abraham and Sarah. Abraham accepted the message that he and Sarah would conceive the promised child, Isaac. Sarah was in the tent and laughed over the Angels announcement to Abraham. She could not believe that she could conceive a son at her age, which was about ninety years old. Even though she didn't believe at first, Sarah did conceive a child, and they named him Isaac. Abraham was about one hundred years old at the start time. Do you suppose that as you become a senior adult God would have a plan for your life too? In the churches of today the senior adults seem to just sit by and listen to the same biblical truths that they have heard many times. The senior adult has so much wisdom to give to a body of believers if they were allowed to share their lives, the teachings, and their wisdom to a growing church. Sometimes the young adults want to turn a deaf ear to these precious saints. The opposite happens when the senior adult feels his time is over to be of any value to a church. Both statements are wrong because as long as you have breath, God has a plan. Remember that God hates a proud attitude.

We met a sixty-five year old lady several years ago who admitted to us that when she was a teenager, she rendered to God's mission work. She soon married right after high school and had four children within five years. Then one dreadful day her husband was riding home on a motorcycle and was killed instantly. She chose to raise her children by herself until they were adults. She always remembered her commitment to God regarding missions, but now she felt she was too old to follow through with the promise she had made when she was a girl. We encouraged her and reminded her that God had not forgotten her prayer and promise she had made to God. She could still fulfill her promise. Several months later we received a letter from her stating that she was going to Russia to teach God's Word for 30 days. She was going with a team, and she was excited that she truly was not too old to be on mission with God. When she returned from Russia, her heart was flying high, spiritually, knowing now that she had not failed God. She did what God had in mind for her to accomplish. She taught several people a lesson and that is, "It never is too late to go with God and be spiritually sensitive to the whispers of the Holy Spirit." We just need to be available to go with God's perfect plan to reach others for Christ.

The senior adult may have had years of hearing God's whispers and he knows the Lord. These powerful saint's are the prayer warrior's that can join all ages to bring glory to God! God has a plan at every age, and we need each other to bring about following God's plan. My prayer is that the prompting of God's whispers overflow within your hearts. He will lift you up!

> *Ephesians 4:11-13, "It was he who gave some to be apostles, some to be prophets, some to be evangelists, and some to be pastors and teachers, to prepare God's people for works of service, so that the body of Christ may be built up until we all reach unity in the faith and in the knowledge of the Son of God and become mature, attaining to the whole measure of the fullness of Christ." NIV*

1. *Pray*
    Lord, teach me humility that directs me to desire to do your will. Help me to be spiritually discerning to your whispers and to surrender to the Holy Spirit working through my life.

2. *Reflection*
    Have you witnessed the desire for God's plan to be accomplished through any age? Does the young saint need to respect the old? Does the older saint need to respect the young? Can we work together to accomplish God's plan?

CHAPTER 7

The Whisper of Grace

L et us take a journey together for a few minutes. You and a friend are both sitting on the steps of a rundown house talking about your future. You both are good friends, and you have been living in a poor community all of your lives. You do not know how to get out of the area you in which you are living and you both are talking about your disappointments about your parents. They are neither at home most of the time, leaving you to fend for your own food, or one of them is drinking your food money away. You are both very hungry and feel doomed to living like this the rest of your lives. Then something strange happens and a long fancy automobile pulls up to the house. The man and woman in the back seat of the car call out your names. You both look at each other and want to run because you have been taught never to speak to strangers, but they asked "Where are your parents?" "In the house" was your reply, so they get out and go into the house. Your mom comes out and tells you both that she had called your friend's mom and that they both agreed that you could go with this couple and that it was safe. You and your friend get in this car with velvet seats and snuggle in for a long drive. You drive through a large rod iron gate and down a long road to a mansion that looks like a castle. Two people come out of the castle to direct you both into different rooms. You each have our own dressers, beds, televisions, and there are clothes laid out for you on the bed. You grumble because you have to take a bath first! You dress yourself, and then there is a knock at the door. You are invited to a luxurious dining room to have lunch. The conversation at the table is welcoming and you are told that this will be your permanent home. You will never again have to worry about the clothes you wear, or you will never go hungry again. You and your friend are now children of the greatest KING that ever lived!

This is the meaning of GRACE because you do nothing to receive what Jesus Christ did for you. You and your friend, who are about twelve years old, are going to take another journey together. There will be another road taken to show you what cost was paid for you to receive this free gift and your name will be whispered. He knows your name. The Holy Spirit was there to witness these events, and He is indwelling every believer today. Join me in seeing through the eyes of the Holy Spirit in what He experienced through two children. This story is fictional, but let us just say that you are one of those children. The story is based on the truth written in the Bible.

The Garden where Jesus Prayed

You and your friend were playing in a beautiful garden and decided to sit on a rock to eat your sack lunch that you brought along to eat. A servant tells you to be home by 4:00 p.m. to prepare you for the evening meal. She asks you to be careful but to have fun. You both hear some commotion as several men approach the garden. One of the men asks the others to wait and pray where they are and he goes on alone to pray. Oh, my goodness, the man is heading to the rock you and your friend are sitting on, so you run to hide behind a large tree to watch to see what happens next. You stand quietly, and you do not dare move. You hear the man begin to talk, but to whom is he talking? You do not see anyone else around.

> *Luke 22:39-44, Jesus went out as usual to the Mount of Olives, and his disciples followed him. On reaching the place, he said to them, "Pray that you will not fall into temptation." He withdrew about a stone's throw beyond them, knelt down and prayed, "Father, if you are willing, take this cup from*

me; yet not my will, but yours be done." An angel from heaven appeared to him and strengthened him. And being in anguish, he prayed more earnestly, and his sweat was like drops of blood falling to the ground. NIV

You become frightened, because another man appears to encourage and strengthen the first man. You notice the man who was talking is bleeding from his face. He looks so unhappy and appears to be in great stress. You and your friend finally realize that this man is praying with deep emotion. His tears flow saying "Not my will, but your will be done." He gently looks in your direction, and he knows you are there watching. He does not move, but continues to pray. Your names are whispered, and you begin to listen closely. You ask each other, "How does he know our names?" He says it again "Not my will, but your will be done." What cup does he not want to drink from? Maybe someone is going to poison him? You say that you would not want to drink poison. This man says he is going to drink it anyway, so that you could be free from punishment for your sins. You are now wondering about what kind of punishment? He is going to die? You continue to listen and you begin to understand that he cares about you and your friend. You both decide that you are going to follow this man to see where he is going to go next. You remember the servant from the mansion who told you to be home by 4:00 p.m., but you cannot obey this time. You are drawn to follow this kind man who knows you are watching. He goes back to the other men are waiting and they have fallen asleep. He asks them why they could not pray for just one hour without him. He heads back to the rock again to pray. You watch for almost three hours. You see this kind man cry out for people who are evil, unkind and do not understand. He has done miracles of healing, raising the dead and people still do not understand. Who was this kind, gentle and powerful man? You both decide that you have to find out for yourselves.

Jesus is Arrested

You follow and watch behind trees. The sun began to set and it became quite dark. You ask each other, "Why are they staying out here for so long?" The kind man told one of the men with him that he would deny him three times before the night was over. He said that a rooster would crow to remind him of what the kind man had told him. I guess they were pretty good friends, because the other man said that he would never deny the kind man. You hear footsteps from a large group of people. This frightens you! They are carrying lights on poles. You begin to see that they are soldiers in armor. The man leading them is not a soldier, but walks up to the man that had been praying for along time. He kissed the kind man on the cheek. The soldiers then grab and hit the kind man in the face. You gasped! What is going on here now? You asked, "Why are these soldiers being so mean?" Then the kind man's friend that was with him took out a sword and cut off one the soldier's ears. You whisper to each as to why you were still there watching? You were curious and were hoping the kind man would escape. He touched the man that had lost an ear and put it back like new. Who is this man?

Luke 22:47-53, And while He was still speaking, behold, a multitude; and he who was called Judas, one of the twelve, went before them and drew near to Jesus to kiss Him. But Jesus said to him, "Judas, are you betraying the Son of Man with a kiss?" When those around Him saw what was going to happen, they said to Him, "Lord, shall we strike with the sword?" And one of them struck the servant of the high priest and cut off his right ear. But Jesus answered and said, "Permit even this." And He touched his ear and healed him. Then Jesus said to the chief priests, captains of the temple, and the elders who had come to Him, "Have you come out, as against a robber, with swords and clubs? When I was with you daily in the temple, you did not try to seize Me. But this is your hour, and the power of darkness." NKJV

You continued to follow, hiding so that no one notices us, to a temple. There are more men that are being mean to this gentle man. The man that was a friend was hiding, too. People saw him in the crowd and kept asking him if he was a follower of the man that was arrested? We saw him with the kind man, but this friend was lying to people and telling that he did not know the man arrested. You turned to ask your friend if he would tell people that he was not your friend. Your friend said, "No, you will always be my friend." Why was this man lying about not knowing his friend? He told three people that he did not know the kind man and then a rooster crowed! Oh, my, goodness, when the man heard the crow, he broke down in tears and ran from the people around him. He felt bad for lying, you thought. But you remembered that the kind man told his friend that would happen. The kind man can tell the future, too! Are these mean men going to give this kind man the cup with poison now? Why would anyone be so ugly with someone that has been so gentle to people?

There seems to be a trial going on in the temple. Why? We listened very closely to hear what was being said. They were not holding cups, but beating this kind man. You and your friend talked about others calling you both ugly names before, and it was not nice. This always made you get mad! This kind man was not getting mad. Why? He told the people around him that he was the Son of God! Wow! We believed him, but the other people did not believe him.

> *Luke 22:63-71, Now the men who held Jesus mocked Him and beat Him. And having blindfolded Him, they struck Him on the face and asked Him, saying, "Prophesy! Who is the one who struck You?" And many other things they blasphemously spoke against Him.*

> ### *Note: Jesus Faces the Sanhedrin*
> ### *(Matt 26:57-68; Mark 14:61-64; John 18:12-14, 19-24)*

> *As soon as it was day, the elders of the people, both chief priests and scribes, came together and led Him into their council, saying, "If You are the Christ, tell us." But He said to them, "If I tell you, you will by no means believe. And if I also ask you, you will by no means answer Me or let Me go. Hereafter the Son of Man will sit on the right hand of the power of God." Then they all said, "Are You then the Son of God?" So He said to them, "You rightly say that I am." And they said,*

"What further testimony do we need? For we have heard it ourselves from His own mouth." NKJV

The bad people decided to take the kind man, after he had already been beaten, to someone called Pontius Pilot. You followed the crowd. You said to your friend that you were getting really tired, because you had not slept all night. Your friend said, in return, "Boy, are we going to get in trouble for staying out all night long!" You both started to cry asking each other why these people were being so terrible. You began remembering how kind this man was when he was praying. He looked at us with such tenderness.

The people said that this kind man was teaching false stories and stirring up the people. Pontius Pilot could not condemn the man, so he sent him to King Herod. King Herod was excited to meet this man, but ended up teasing him. He put on a mock robe and sent him back to Pontius Pilot. Why was this entire thing going on? It seemed like an awful drama taking place, but it was real! Neither Pontius Pilot nor King Herod could find this kind man guilty of any wrongdoing. He did not deserve death. You and your friend were confused as to why these grown men were accusing this man. What was so bad about his teaching? Pilate had this kind and gentle man beaten again, but why was this man not mad at them? Why did he not defend himself? Why did he not say he was innocent? Why wasn't anybody standing up for him? Why was the crowd so angry when he had shown them such care? Why? He had healed their sick! He had raised their loved ones from the dead. Why? The anger was out of control and you both wanted to run from this madness. You both could not get through the number of people that were gathering together. Pilot allowed another man to be released due to a certain day of the year, because the religious leaders wanted an evil man released instead of this gentle man. You did not understand. They began to cry out, "Crucify Him"! Two men grabbed each of your arms and asked why you were not crying out? They asked us if we wanted to be "Crucified, too?" You were scared, so you began crying out, too. Tears were rolling down your cheeks, because your heart was breaking. How many other people felt this same way? Maybe other people were being threatened if they did not agree with the Chief Priests and church leaders. You did not know for sure, but you knew you did not agree to what was happening. I guess this was the cup of poison that this man prayed would not have to happen, but he was willing to die so that you would not be punished for your sins. The whisper was gently heard in your heart that said "The wages of sin is death." The reality is that we should all be punished for allowing this evil to happen.

> *Luke 23:18-26, And they all cried out at once, saying, "Away with this Man, and release to us Barabbas" — who had been thrown into prison for a certain rebellion made in the city, and for murder. Pilate, therefore, wishing to release Jesus, again called out to them. 21 But they shouted, saying, "Crucify Him, crucify Him!" Then he said to them the third time, "Why, what evil has He done? I have found no reason for death in Him. I will therefore chastise Him and let Him go." But they were insistent, demanding with loud voices that He be crucified. And the voices of these men and of the chief priests prevailed. So Pilate gave sentence that it should be as they requested. And he released to them the one they requested, who for rebellion and murder had been thrown into prison; but he delivered Jesus to their will. NKJV*

Jesus carries His Cross

You and your friend began watching the soldiers put a crown of terrible thorns on the head of the kind man. He had been beaten so badly. You could not recognize him as a man. You cried and you both decided you didn't want to see anything more, but suddenly the servant from the house showed up standing next to you. She was not angry, but hurting with tears of her own running down her face. She was so thankful that she had found you. She told you that she needed to follow this man down the road to where he was going to be crucified. She did not want either of you to leave her side, but stay close to her all the way. She covered her head and joined a group of other women who began to slowly walk close to the kind man carrying a rugged heavy piece of wood. We had never witnessed this before and it was awful. The women were crying and wailing. The kind man told them not to cry for him, but for themselves and their children. He continued to walk, but became very weak. The rugged piece of wood could have been 70 pounds heavy. That would be difficult for a strong man to carry, but not this gentle man that had been beaten on his face, back and legs. The soldiers pulled a man out of the crowd, that was watching, telling him to carry the cross now. Our servant lady called out "Simon"! It was so long a journey. The road was rocky and dusty. You and your friend were slowly walking watching this man struggle to take one more step. He glanced over to look at you through bloodied beaten eyes, but they were still tender. He had no anger, no self-pity, and no regret showing in his eyes. You ask yourself, "How can this man be so different, yet still caring, then most men? Who is this man? Why is he not crying out in pain? He said he would drink this cup so that you would not be punished. You are thinking that you should be punished for doing what you have done to this humble man. You know that he is a very good person. You have not heard him say a negative word. You remember him telling the men that followed him to pray and not fall a sleep so that they would not fall into temptation. You begin to pray as you take another step along this dark rocky road. You feel a sudden urgency that you must follow this man from this day forward. You want to hear from others what he has been teaching. You are being changed and do not understand what this feeling is about. You are feeling deep guilt, but there is a hint of joy in the middle of what you are experiencing. (Luke 23:26-28)

Jesus Dies and Rises Again

> *John 19:17-22, And He, bearing His cross, went out to a place called the Place of a Skull, which is called in Hebrew, Golgotha, where they crucified Him, and two others with Him, one on either side, and Jesus in the center. 19 Now Pilate wrote a title and put it on the cross. And the writing was: JESUS OF NAZARETH, THE KING OF THE JEWS. Then many of the Jews read this title, for the place where Jesus was crucified was near the city; and it was written in Hebrew, Greek, and Latin. Therefore the chief priests of*

the Jews said to Pilate, "Do not write, 'The King of the Jews,'
but, 'He said, "I am the King of the Jews.""' Pilate answered,
"What I have written, I have written." NKJV

This kind man's name was Jesus, because you began to hear his name over and over. He struggled to walk the hill to Golgotha. When he reached the top of the hill, the soldiers threw him to the ground. They then placed him on to a wooden pole that was on the ground. There were two other men being placed on two other wooden poles. One pole was located on each side of Jesus, but these two other men were being tied on the wooden beams with ropes. Oh, my, gosh, Jesus was being nailed to the wooden beam! Oh, NO!! The soldiers were hammering nails into his hands and feet and he never cursed anyone. The anguish that you were feeling was hard to describe. Your friend was hiding behind the skirt of the woman servant. He was not watching anything that was going on, but you could not take your eyes off the man that was so kind and gentle. There was several soldiers that lifted him up and slammed the wooden pole into a hole in the ground. You heard him yell out and then you looked away for a moment. Your stomach was beginning to hurt and you could not control the tears that were coming down your cheek. You saw a woman and a man standing at the foot of the cross when Jesus began to speak to them. He said something to the woman, which sounded, "Woman behold your son". The he slightly turned to the man and said "Behold your mother." He told the soldiers that he was thirsty, so they put something to his mouth that was bitter. He turned away from the sponge that was attached to a spear.

Then the man looked directly at you and whispered, " I am willing to die for you, so that you can be free of punishment and have your sins forgiven for all eternity." No one else heard what he had said to you personally. You believed him and experienced a peace you have never had. You heard him cry out "It is finished!" He bowed his head gave up his spirit." He died! A soldier took a long spear and pierces him in the side to make sure he was not alive. Out flowed blood and water from this man's stomach. Then I heard another soldier cry out "Surely this was the Son of God!" The earth began to shake and the black clouds covered the area. You, your friend and the lady servant began to run! You were not going to stop running until you got back to the castle. You ran past the temple and it was breaking apart. You were all frightened and kept running. You finally reached the castle and closed the doors behind you. You ran to your room and slammed the door hiding under the covers. No one came into your room, so you just lay there for hours. The night fell and you went to sleep.

The next day you and everyone in the castle stayed inside not wanting to venture outside for fear of what they might see. What just happened, "you ask yourself?" Sunday was the next day and people were just barely moving around in the house. There was a knock at the front door whispering news that began to excite the one that answered the door. He is alive! You ask, "Who is alive?" The answer is the kind man who was crucified! You asked how he could be alive unless he was "God!" Yes, the message was spreading all over the countryside that Jesus was alive! People were sharing that they had seen him, but you had not seen him yet. You secretly thought, "What a blessing it would be if you could see him."

You and your friend see that the difficult times are simmering down. The house becomes busy again and meals are served on time. You and your friend are not afraid to go outside again, but you are not going back to the garden to play. The fenced back yard seems to be a better place to play. The servant woman calls you in to meet the KING, the owner of the castle. You had never met him before and they did say that you and your friend were his children now. You both are directed into the parlor of the house. You walk in and there stands JESUS with His arms open wide! You run to him and jump into His arms. GRACE has been revealed to you! You have done nothing to deserve His love and commitment to provide for you the greatest gift that will ever be given.

Grace Whispers your Name

> *Ephesians 2:1-10, And you He made alive, who were dead in trespasses and sins, in which you once walked according to the course of this world, according to the prince of the power of the air, the spirit who now works in the sons of disobedience, among whom also we all once conducted ourselves in the lusts of our flesh, fulfilling the desires of the flesh and of the mind, and were by nature children of wrath, just as the*

others. But God, who is rich in mercy, because of His great love with which He loved us, even when we were dead in trespasses, made us alive together with Christ (by grace you have been saved), and raised us up together, and made us sit together in the heavenly places in Christ Jesus, that in the ages to come He might show the exceeding riches of His grace in His kindness toward us in Christ Jesus. For by grace you have been saved through faith, and that not of yourselves; it is the gift of God, not of works, lest anyone should boast. For we are His workmanship, created in Christ Jesus for good works, which God prepared beforehand that we should walk in them. NKJV

How could anyone express the meaning of grace as well as the scriptures has done in the book of Ephesians? The work and commitment of Jesus Christ opened a pathway of blessings to those who have chosen to believe. He knew who would believe, but you and others must humble your hearts in obedience to the grace offered to you. You may ask "If Jesus knows who would believe, then why should you share your love for Christ with others?" You may be the vessel that the Holy Spirit has chosen to work through to touch another person's heart. You are God's workmanship, created in Christ Jesus to do good works, which He has prepared for you to do. God has a plan, and He has always had a plan. He desires a relationship with those who choose to believe with a humble heart. He will lift you up in the fullness of God's time. You, nor I, can ever repay Jesus for His sacrificial death on the cross by any works that we do. We are unconditionally loved and accepted. Isn't that what we have always wanted in our journey through life? Jesus Christ has whispered your name! He desires to bless you with His gentle whisper of GRACE. You have done nothing to merit complete forgiveness, but you will receive it as you confess your sin. Have you done something you feel He cannot forgive? When you desire to be forgiven for the worst thing that you have done and humble your heart before a Holy God, you will be forgiven and be changed for the better. Run and jump up into Jesus Christ's open arms. He will catch you!

1. *Pray:*

Lord, please allow me to reflect on what you did for me that has given me the GRACE I do not deserve. Nothing that I could ever do that might glorify you would match what you did for me as you walked to Calvary and died for my sin.

2. *Reflection:*

Do you sense the love that Jesus Christ has given for you? Think about the freedom that you now have because of the GRACE He has offered you.

CHAPTER 8

The Whisper in God's Word

Words can encourage, words can destroy, words bring understanding and words teach. Words are spoken through different languages. Can you envision people speaking to each other like a child to his or her mother, a mother to a child or a husband to his wife? A deaf person speaks with their hands to another deaf person. Communication is the best way we can get to know an individual. Girls seem to chatter and chatter. Boys seem to be somewhat quieter. Someone told me if you spell out the words listen and silent, they use the same letters. Listening can become an art, and you gain knowledge about a subject that you are interested in. You can learn how to drive a car or fly an airplane. We have several different ways that we receive communication and that is through television, through radio and through our cell phones. People call us on our telephones and sometimes stop to visit. Some people read books. When we get excited about something, we will want to tell everybody we know. Today it is Facebook! We want to know what's happening in our world, so we listen to the news. There are so many different ways to communicate and the words keep going on and on. We talk to ourselves. Some people talk to people just to hear their own voice. Everybody has an opinion about something. Did you ever think that the sound of the ocean speaks of life? Do you stop to listen to your child who is crying?

Have you played a game where you just stood still to listen to everything around you? What do you hear? Does the silence bother you? Keep listening! Oh my, you hear your dog barking. Is there knocking on your door, or is your house silent? You step outside and hear the birds calling to each other. The birds speak their own language, so do the squirrels, and so do the chipmunks.

God created and designed you to have communication one with other people. God wants to speak to you with words that you will grow to understand. The modern day man or woman refers to the Holy Bible as the Word of God. What does that mean? God speaks through the Bible. The Bible is not so much about people communicating to God as much as it is about God communicating to man. You need to rise above your own thoughts and see God what has been saying through the passed centuries. The Lord never changes and He is pure and holy. He created you and knew you before you where born.

The message of Jesus Christ is woven through out the entire word of God. He is the thread of truth that binds together all sixty-six chapters together. In the beginning there was God. Listen for the whispers that God has revealed already to humanity.

In the beginning God created

> *Genesis 1:1-2, In the beginning God created the heavens and the earth. Now the earth was formless and empty, darkness was over the surface of the deep, and the Spirit of God was hovering over the waters. NIV*

The next few verses of the Scripture says, "And God said" and they are found in verse(s) 3, 6, 9, 14, 20, 24 and 29 of the first chapter. The second chapter it is found in 2:18 and the third chapter it is found in 3:13. When God speaks, should you listen? The human mind passes by the most important message of all, and that is that God spoke everything into existence. He finished preparing the earth for man to exist and live comfortably. He created man and woman in His image. God blessed them and spoke to them! You mean to tell me that He spoke to the humans he created? What were the words that He spoke?

God wanted to protect the man and the woman, so 'He said' not to eat of the fruit in the middle of the garden. Why? This fruit would introduce another voice that the man and woman should not listen to because his voice was the voice of destruction. God gave mankind the ability to make choices. The voice of destruction was a smooth talker, and he appealed to their immature desires. Self-centeredness was birthed into the human heart. This dark voice introduced sin that would start a rebellion against the God that created all of life. His voice is darkness and God's whisper is the light. The first war that a man or woman would fight is light against darkness.

Genesis is the book that begins the relationship that God desires for a man or a woman to have with Him, but a jealous fallen created being wants to continue to destroy that bonded spiritual relationship. Does he exist today? Yes, he does, but we have victory by having a relationship with God through the Word of God. Do you understand why we should not read the words of man through the Scriptures? Let us, you and I, begin a journey through the Scripture and listen carefully to what God has whispered to a man or woman. You have just read what God said and all of life was born. Let us go a little further in the Scriptures.

What happened to the serpent who is the dark voice that is God's enemy.

> *Genesis 3:14-15, So the Lord God said to the serpent, "Because you have done this, "Cursed are you above all the livestock and all the wild animals! You will crawl on your belly and you will eat dust all the days of your life. And I will put enmity between you and the woman, and between your offspring and hers; he will crush your head, and you will strike his heel." NIV*

Who will crush the enemy's heel? Is this the first whisper of Jesus Christ, the Savior to be born? Have you missed the message? The first sin introduced a new plan to draw a man or a woman back to God. It does not take God a long time to create another plan to win the heart of His people. The nature of God is that He can break down any brick wall that is planted before Him, but He may take the time to allow a man or a woman to understand what He has spoken. Should you stay stiff-necked and not believe? Well, it may take a long time for God's whispers to be heard by you. What can happen if God is angry and what would be the reason?

God Ends Human Life

> *Genesis 6:11-13, Now the earth was corrupt in God's sight and was full of violence. God saw how corrupt the earth had become, for all the people on earth had corrupted their ways. So God said to Noah, "I am going to put an end to all people, for the earth is filled with violence because of them, I am surely going to destroy both them and the earth. NIV*

Who was Noah that God would speak to him like He did? Noah was a righteous and blameless man among his people. He walked with God and heard the whispers that came from God on a daily basis. God won the heart of Noah. (Genesis 6:9-10) God told Noah to build an ark and gave precise measurements on how big this ark should be able to house many animals. God chose to bless and save Noah's immediate family, too. This was because of the faithful heart that Noah had for his God. God became angry at the attitude and actions of the people that he had created. They became violent, uncaring, self-centered, stealing from other people and sacrificing their own children. They were listening to the voice of the serpent and this was not wisdom. The knowledge of good and evil was going rampant. Only one man and his family were acknowledging God as the creator and had a relationship with Him. God was teaching this one man to be honorable and caring of other people. God was about to pronounce judgment on the earth.

Today, we have the same problem, and the knowledge of good and evil is running rampant. What makes you and me think that we are not going to be judged? The television programs are violent and seem to lift up the criminal. The news broadcasts are always reporting the bad news of what people deliver to our world. Children are being abducted and murdered. Women are being raped and sometimes murdered. Husbands are murdering their families and putting fire to their homes. Jobs are not available for people to take care of their families. People are stealing to support their drugs habits. Young girls are being abducted for human trafficking. This is sin, and this angers God!

Do you think just maybe if we would return back to a God believing nation that He may bless us? God honored this nation for many years because of the faithful. People laugh in God's face saying, "His rules are too hard to follow." His rules are not hard to follow with the help of God's Holy Spirit. Our nation is a nation of many religions, and that's what happened to Israel before it was sent into bondage. Some of what has happened in our nation is due to the evil disobedience of generations past. King Solomon welcomed other religions and started to practice those religions. His kingdom was divided after his death and has never been one nation again. Disobedience costs us our freedom. Can you agree that our nation is experiencing God's discipline? We seem to want more all the time, and we don't care if people go hungry. God has given us his grace and His mercy. The true believers need to pray to welcome God's power to over take the evil that is present. Our churches need to be filled with people seeking the heart of God and not seeking personal recognition. He will bless our nation if we call on the Lord to change our hearts, our wants, our personal desires, and our self-centered attitudes. God did promise that he would never destroy the earth again with the flood because he wants us to return to Him. How can you not surrender to the pure love of God? You need to know that he will provide for you, that he has a plan for you and that He wants to give you a new life. Noah followed God's instructions, and his family was saved. His heart was saddened that so many people had perished, but he did not have control regarding the choices they made. He only had control over his relationship to God. He encouraged people to believe, but they chose not to believe. Because they chose not to believe, judgment fell and a price was paid.

Would you join with me to pray for spiritual revival for our nation? Would you join with me to make the choice to grow in a closer relationship with God? Would you join with me to tell the truth of who God is and what Jesus did for them? Has he whispered to your heart to make a difference in your part of the world? Listen to his still small voice. Lift up the name of Jesus! The greatest blessing is that God will remember your name, so let Him lift you up as you glorify Him! Has God spoken to humanity about His displeasure regarding sin? Has He whispered to your heart? God reveals His message through Abraham in our next section. God has the choice to birth life and to take life, for He created the heavens and the earth. A healthy fear and respect for God is the beginning of wisdom.

Offer Your Son as a Sacrifice

> *Genesis 22:2, Then God said, "Take your son, your only son, Isaac, whom you love, and go to the region of Moriah. Sacrifice him there as a burnt offering on one of the mountains I will tell you about." NIV*

God said, "What?" Can you believe that God actually asked Abraham to sacrifice his only son Isaac? What kind of God do we have that he would ask Abraham to do such a thing? Is God really that insensitive to a man that loves his son? Abraham waited until he was 100 years old to finally have the son God promised him. It's amazing that he even had a son at 100 years old. His wife was 90 years old. She had never had any children and now God was going to break her heart, too? There is a secret to all of this as you continue to read. Abraham had made a commitment in his heart to never disobey God again, so he was willing to sacrifice his son. His heart grew to hear the whispers of God throughout his life. He knew what God wanted him to do without question. Can you imagine taking a long hike up the mountain knowing that you were going to sacrifice your only son on an altar to God? You would be grieving within your heart, but you knew that God had a message through this, so you became obedient. Abraham told his son to join him to sacrifice a lamb. When Abraham and Isaac started up the mountain, Isaac asked where the sacrificial lamb was. Abraham looked at his son and said, "God will provide." When they prepared the altar, Abraham began to wrap his son to be sacrificed. Isaac trusted Abraham, so he surrendered to the love of his father. Just as Abraham lifted his knife to slay Isaac, God stopped him. God said if you are so willing to sacrifice your only son I know that you entrusted me with the very thing you have love the most. God provided the lamb for the sacrifice, and it would not be Isaac. The plan and message of redemption began with the obedience of Abraham. God's plan was being revealed to you and to mankind. The heart of God was touched by the obedience of Abraham, and God lifted Abraham up. God also blessed Isaac due to Abraham's obedience.

Will God ever ask you to sacrifice something that you love? What do you love the most? Do you love the home that you live in, or the car you drive, or the job you have? Do you love where you are living right now? Do you love your children, your parents, your brothers and sisters? Are you willing to go wherever God asked you to go without a promise of an income to provide for your family? Are you willing to give up all your material possessions to live in poverty? Do you believe that God will provide if he asked you to do something? Is your relationship with God first in your life? Will you sacrifice what you love the most when God asks you to do something? Do you believe that God has a plan to work through your life and bless you for your obedience? We can never out give God! Abraham was just a man, but he was a man of faith. Are you looking at the person, or are you looking at God's character? Do you really think that God wanted to harm the young boy? The most important question is how God related to it Abraham. He promised him many blessings, and this will be shared in another chapter. God wants to reveal himself to the human heart, and he wants to bless those who would believe. God Himself would eventually sacrifice his own son for you. His heart would be broken because he loves you and he loves me. You are so special to him. Do you feel, through the power of the Holy Spirit, His love? What have the whispers of God been telling you? There are no sacrifices more than what God has already given to you that you should be frightened. When you take the step of faith that He may asking you to take, you will learn more about God than you ever thought you would. Walk that path, choose to be obedient, and you will experience what I am trying to share with you.

The Promise

> *Jeremiah 29:10-14, "This is what the Lord says: 'When*
> *seventy years are completed for Babylon, I will come to you*
> *and fulfill my gracious promise to bring you back to this place.*
> *For I know the plans I have for you,' declares the Lord, 'plans*
> *to prosper you and not to harm you, plans to give you hope*
> *and a future. Then you will call upon me and come and pray*
> *to me, and I will listen to you. You will seek me and find me*
> *when you seek me with all your heart. I will be found by you,'*
> *declares the Lord, 'and will bring you back from captivity. I*
> *will gather you from all the nations and places where I have*
> *banished you,' declares the Lord, 'and will bring you back to*
> *the place from which I carried you into exile.'" NIV*

The people of Israel had sinned against God, so he allowed the people to be put in captivity in Babylon. God does discipline his people, but he also makes promises. God spoke through Jeremiah the prophet and told the people to have families, build their homes and be at peace in the land where they were living. Remember what I told you earlier in this chapter that it's not about the people, but it is about God's character and how He relates to humanity? Can you see how loving and provisional God can be to the people He created and called his own? You've seen several plaques with a Scripture that says, "I know the plans I have for you", declares the Lord, "plans to prosper you and not harm you, plans to give you hope and a future?" Do you think that these Scriptures are a permanent promise to believers today? You already know that these word(s) were written for the people of Israel, but what about today? God gave instructions that we, as believers, can call on God and pray, and that He will listen. Is that true today? If you seek him with all of your heart, you will find him. He has taught these word(s) to His people through all generations.

Do you sometimes sense that God does not hear your prayers? The prayer hits the ceiling and does not go beyond? First, you have to confess your sin because God does not like sin. Remember the flood and why God destroyed humanity? Now you see God forgiving again, after he sent his people into captivity in Babylon. He forgives over and over the sins his people commit. He promises to provide, to love, and to give a brighter future to those who believe. These Scriptures are an encouragement to those who belong to God. Isn't it wonderful that God said that He would prosper you? It's fabulous that He would not harm you, and give you hope and a future. Trust his word(s) for your future. Seek the Lord with all of your heart, and you will find Him.

The peace of God's Holy Spirit, that is in believers, is what balances relationships in our world today. Each life that belongs to God's is a touch of God's hand in our world of darkness. You are needed to assist in bringing the light to the world. Do you hear the Holy Spirit whisper these promises to your heart?

We are just attempting to skim the surface of what God has said through the Scriptures. Try and do a word study on what God has said by viewing a concordance of your choice. One example is when God spoke to Moses at the burning bush. (Exodus 3:12-14). God spoke to Solomon after He prayed. (II Chronicles 1:11) There are so many examples in the Old Testament that you can find as you do this word study. It is amazing how God did speak in the Word of God to people! I am thankful for the people who have recorded these encounters they had with God. He has revealed who He is and how He wants to assist and protect His people.

The Word was God

> *John 1:1-6, In the beginning was the Word, and the Word was with God, and the Word was God. He was with God in the beginning. Through him all things were made; without him nothing was made that has been made. In him was life, and that life was the light of men. The light shines in the darkness, but the darkness has not understood it.*

In the beginning was the word, and the Word was God himself! God became flesh and walked among men. God had a plan for humanity to get right with him again. Jesus was born to open the door for people to a have personal relationship with a Holy God. The darkness did not know him, and people were confused. Who was this man? He brought spiritual enlightenment to God's law that He gave centuries before. You can't even imagine the sacrifices He has made for those that would choose to believe. He left the glory of heaven and His throne to become human.

There is an example about why God did what he did. This is a simple fictional story. I don't know who told the story, but it's about a flock of birds. It was getting close to the first snowfall of the season. These birds did not fly south in time for winter. They saw a warm fire glowing, so they headed towards that fire. The little birds hit something hard and fell to the ground. Some of those birds were killed, but some were not injured. The birds flew again towards the fire and hit the windowpane again. There was a man inside sitting in front of the fire and noticed that the little birds were trying to get into where he was. He stepped outside and began waving his arms to try to get the little birds to fly away. The birds did not understand the man's communication to them, so they kept flying into the window. The man went back to sit in his chair concerned for those little birds. He was wondering how he could communicate with them to let them know what they were doing was harming them. Then he thought to himself and said, "If I only could become a bird, just for a little while, then I could tell them what they were doing was harmful to them". This man realized that's what Jesus did for us because God the father was trying to communicate to humanity saying, "You're destroying yourself, you're hurting yourself and the people would not listen." So God chose to become a man speaking directly to people, but some still did not understand. Those that choose not to understand will perish. It is not God's will for anyone to perish. It is man's choice to believe or not to believe, and this has been true since heaven and earth were created. The Garden of Eden was God's initial plan, but man did make a choice. It is your choice to believe, to become spiritually sensitive to the Holy Spirit's whispers to your heart and to serve God with your time, talent and money that God has provided.

The Word was with God, the Word was God and the Word walked among men. The Word is the Alpha and Omega, which is the beginning and the end. Are you listening to the Word of God?

What is your name? Your mother and father gave you your name. God knows your name and sees you through the veil of a sacrificial lamb that was sacrificed for you on the Cross of Calvary. If you are a believer, then the Holy Father does not remember your sins, but if you are not a believer, you will die in your sins. You will be separated for all eternity from a God that loves you. Choose today to believe and be made right with the one true God. Prayer opens the path to communication to your heart. Jesus has told you that you must be born spiritually. It is like watching the effects of the wind. You cannot see the wind, but you can feel the wind on your face. Let the fresh warm wind of the Holy Spirit penetrate your heart with the truth of God's love. Listen for His whispers!

1.   *Pray:*

Lord, I am so thankful for the inspired writers that have given humanity the words that have come from your heart. These writings have given us an understanding of your character and how you consistently you seek fellowship with mankind. Thank you for including me and instructing me through the Word of God.

2.   *Reflection:*

Are you listening for God's whispers when you read the scriptures? Has your heart been touched by the truth that God's Holy Spirit wants revealed?

CHAPTER 9

The Whisper through Angels

T he title of this chapter may have taken you by surprise, but I
believe as we continue how to learn to recognize the small still
voice of God you will understand why I chose this subject. All
through the centuries there have been pictures painted of winged creatures
that are human looking. The Sistine Chapel in Rome, Italy, has several
pictures showing a baby or child looking winged creatures. I know that
you can purchase pictures and little statues like this in several stores today.
People started giving me the statues as gifts several years ago and still do.
These winged creatures are called Cherubim. Where did the information
get started that angels have wings? Are Cherubim and Angels the same?
When reading the scriptures I find that Cherubim seem to be symbolic
in nature. God has His purpose for the Cherubim, and I will not dispute
their existence or God's design for the service they provide Him. Do angels
exist today? What is the purpose of an angel? There was a television sitcom
called "Touched by an Angel" that was seen every week for several years.
Do angels enter into a relationship with people like these stories tell us? I
believe that the best place for us to start is in the Word of God. I want to
look at the encounters that people had in the scriptures to find out what
their purpose was in relationship to people. I want you to open your mind,
but not too far because Satan has appeared in the form of an angel. We
have been told that he is a fallen angel who rebelled against God. Has an

experience with a possible angel been comforting or frightening to you? Billy Graham wrote an entire book called *Angels Unaware*. There have been experiences that have been written that share that angels do exist. I will walk you through the Old Testament to reveal three angel experiences and then through three experiences in the New Testament. I will then reveal one of my own experiences with you at the very end of this chapter. I pray that you focus on what God will whisper to you comparing it to what the Bible has already said. Please, continue to rest in the Lord.

> *Hebrews 13:1-2, "Keep on loving each other as brothers. Do not forget to entertain strangers, for by so doing some people have entertained angels without knowing it." NIV*

The Whisper to Hagar

Who was Hagar and why would an angel of the Lord speak to her as she is running from Sarai? Let us go back to the previous time in the scriptures to reveal what had happened. Hagar was the personal Egyptian maidservant to Sarai who was the wife of Abraham. Sarai gave Hagar to become a wife to Abraham because God had promised a descendent to Abraham and Sarai, but Sarai had not yet conceived the baby. Sarai had a problem with trusting God's timing for this promised child, so she took the issue into her own hands to resolve and offered Hagar to Abraham. Hagar conceived, and she then began to despise Sarai. Sarai came to Abraham complaining about Hagar's attitude towards her, and then Abraham told her to do what she wanted to with Hagar. Sarai was jealous and began to mistreat Hagar miserably, so Hagar ran away into the desert. Here are the scriptures that tell of her encounter with an angel.

> *Genesis 16:7-14, Now the Angel of the Lord found her by a spring of water in the wilderness, by the spring on the way to Shur. And He said, "Hagar, Sarai's maid, where have you come from, and where are you going?" She said, "I am fleeing from the presence of my mistress Sarai." The Angel of the Lord said to her, "Return to your mistress, and submit yourself under her hand." Then the Angel of the Lord said to her, "I*

will multiply your descendants exceedingly, so that they shall not be counted for multitude." And the Angel of the Lord said to her: "Behold, you are with child, And you shall bear a son. You shall call his name Ishmael, Because the Lord has heard your affliction. He shall be a wild man; His hand shall be against every man, And every man's hand against him. And he shall dwell in the presence of all his brethren." Then she called the name of the Lord who spoke to her, You-Are-the-God-Who-Sees; for she said, "Have I also here seen Him who sees me?" Therefore the well was called Beer Lahai Roi; observe, it is between Kadesh and Bered. NKJV

Hagar did as the Angel of the Lord told her to do because the Lord saw her misery and protected the birth of her son. She bore Abraham a son and named him Ishmael. Abraham was eighty-six years old when Ishmael was born. There was more mentioned later in the scripture regarding Hagar after this encounter with the angel. Why did the angel appear to Hagar, and what purpose did that the angel fulfill? Did you notice that there is no gender given to the angel or a name? The angel of the Lord found Hagar and then asked her a question. When she responded, then the angel gave her the message from the Lord. The angel told her to go back to Sarai and that she would give birth to a son. Do you suppose she could have been humbled with this encounter? There is no mention of the angel having wings in these scriptures. The next time that Hagar was mentioned was after the promised son of Abraham and Sarai was born and then weaned. Abraham was promised that through his son Isaac a great nation would come because he was the promised son given by God. Hagar's son began to mock the celebration planned for Isaac, so Sarai again asked Abraham to get rid of Hagar and her son. Abraham became distressed because the boy was his son, too. The Lord promised Abraham that his son through Hagar would become a nation, but it was not the promised inheritance that would come through Isaac. Abraham sent Hagar and her son on their way into the desert with the provision of food and water. Hagar ran out of water and then placed the boy under a bush thinking that he would soon die, but the angel of the Lord came to Hagar once again.

Genesis 21:17-21, God heard the boy crying, and the angel of God called to Hagar from heaven and said to her, "What is the matter, Hagar? Do not be afraid; God has heard the boy crying as he lies there. Lift the boy up and take him by the hand, for I will make him into a great nation." Then God opened her eyes and she saw a well of water. So she went and filled the skin with water and gave the boy a drink. God was with the boy as he grew up. He lived in the desert and became an archer. While he was living in the Desert of Paran, his mother got a wife for him from Egypt. NIV

This last time the angel spoke to Hagar from heaven and did not appear in any kind of form. I just want to express to you what we learn from the Bible is the true source of what angels are asked to do by God. Listen and read carefully. The reasons for angels are to be God's messengers as whispered from God.

The Whisper to Balaam

Who am I that God could work through me to help change my part of the world? The Lord clearly states in His word that we are not to think more highly of ourselves than we ought to when we are teachers of the Word of God. I am reminded that if the Lord would cause a donkey to speak, then God could work through me. My pastor husband said that the story of Balaam is a serious but fun story of how an angel of the Lord sent a different kind of message. The Hebrew people had been fighting to obtain the Promised Land that was to be their inheritance given to them by God. In Numbers 22 the Israelites had finally reached the plains of Moab and camped along the Jordan across from Jericho. There was a man named Balak son of Zippor who had witnessed and heard of the strength of these people, and he was frightened. The Bible said that he was terrified because there were so many people. He did not want the land he was living in to be destroyed, so he sent a message to Balaam son of Beor to come to his aid by cursing these people. Balak was the current King of Moab. The message was delivered with Balaam telling them that he must consult the

Lord in prayer. The Lord asked who the men were that were with him? He told them they were messengers for Balak and they asked him to go with them to curse the people Israel. The Lord told Balaam not to go with them and not to put a curse on His people. He further told Balaam that these people were blessed. He got up the next morning to tell the princes that he could not go with them to place a curse on the people that he had been asked to do.

Balak received the return message and was full of anxiety, so he sent another message promising him riches for this service. Balaam prayed again to the Lord, and this time he was told by the Lord to go with them. He was told to do only what the Lord commanded him to do. The Lord became angry because Balaam got up the next morning, saddled his donkey and left with the princes. I believe that Balaam just left without the instructions. He was moving ahead of when the Lord wanted him to go. How many times do we just jump and run without knowing what we are supposed to do next? My thoughts were that maybe Balaam became motivated with the riches that were being offered by King Balak. Here comes an angel to stop Balaam, but he did not see him or hear him speak to him personally at the beginning. His donkey he was riding saw the angel.

Numbers 22:22-35, Then God's anger was aroused because he went, and the Angel of the Lord took His stand in the way as an adversary against him. And he was riding on his donkey, and his two servants were with him. Now the donkey saw the Angel of the Lord standing in the way with His drawn sword in His hand, and the donkey turned aside out of the way and went into the field. So Balaam struck the donkey to turn her back onto the road. Then the Angel of the Lord stood in a narrow path between the vineyards, with a wall on this side and a wall on that side. And when the donkey saw the Angel of the Lord, she pushed herself against the wall and crushed Balaam's foot against the wall; so he struck her again. Then the Angel of the Lord went further, and stood in a narrow place where there was no way to turn either to the right hand or to the left. And when the donkey saw the Angel of the Lord, she lay down under Balaam; so Balaam's anger was aroused, and he struck the donkey with his staff. Then the Lord opened the mouth of the donkey, and she said to Balaam, "What have I done to you, that you have struck me these three times?" And Balaam said to the donkey, "Because you have abused me. I wish there were a sword in my hand, for now I would kill you!" So the donkey said to Balaam, "Am I not your donkey on which you have ridden, ever since I became yours, to this day? Was I ever disposed to do this to you?" And he said, "No." Then the Lord opened Balaam's eyes, and he saw the Angel of the Lord standing in the way with His drawn sword in His hand; and he bowed his head and fell flat on his face. And the Angel of the Lord said to him, "Why have you struck your donkey these three times? Behold, I have come out to stand against you, because your way is perverse before Me. The donkey saw Me and turned aside from Me these three times. If she had not turned aside from Me, surely I would also have killed you by now, and let her live." And Balaam said to the Angel of the Lord, "I have sinned, for I did not know You stood in the way against me. Now therefore, if it displeases You, I will turn back." Then the Angel of the Lord said to Balaam, "Go with the men, but only the word that I speak to you, that you shall speak." NKJV

The message that the Lord gave Balaam to give to Balak was that he could never curse the Israelites, but only to bless them. He blessed the people three times in the presence of King Balak. This angered the King, but he knew he could not get Balaam to do what he had asked him to do. Balaam did not receive the riches that were offered to him, because he did what the Lord told him instead of what was originally asked of him to do from King Balak. The people of God were blessed and would never be cursed. This was made clear through the words spoken through Balaam. I believe seeing the angel with a sword made Balaam obedient to the Lord's command!

Why did the Lord get angry? Why did Balaam not see the angel that the Lord had sent right away? The angel was carrying a sword! This messenger was not pleased, but was still sent by God to carry His message.

Nothing was said about what he looked like, but the angel's message was very precise and direct. The ultimate desire of God was to protect His people and to make sure that other nations knew that He was with them. The Lord God will work through His angels to whisper His clear messages in whatever way He chooses.

Daniel in a Lion's Den

Daniel was a man of prayer who had the favor of God with him. Daniel was in captivity in Babylon and lived during the time of Darius, the new king of the Babylonians. There were 120 satraps that were assigned to rule throughout the kingdom, and Daniel was one of these who had been assigned. His faith in God separated him significantly among these men. They became jealous, because the king favored him. The other satraps devised a plan to get rid of Daniel by a recommendation made to the king. They called out "long live the king!" and said that there needed to be a law put in place to demand that the people pray only to the king for the next thirty days. The decree stated the punishment was that whoever did not pray to the king would be thrown in the lion's den. The king's ego was lifted, and he agreed to this great honor. The king sealed this decree, and the temporary law went into effect. Daniel never changed a habit of praying to his God every day from an open window where people could easily see what he was doing. Daniel was caught and was brought before King Darius. The king was shaken that his decree was going to destroy his favored satrap. He allowed the punishment, but said to Daniel that he hoped his God would save him. Daniel was thrown in the lion's den and a large stone covered the den for security. The king did not sleep at all during the night. He ran to the den the next morning to see what had happened to Daniel and called out to Daniel.

> *Daniel 6:21-23 "Daniel answered, "O king, live forever! My God sent his angel, and he shut the mouths of the lions. They have not hurt me, because I was found innocent in his sight. Nor have I ever done any wrong before you, O king." The king was overjoyed and gave orders to lift Daniel out of the*

den. And when Daniel was lifted from the den, no wound was found on him, because he had trusted in his God." NIV

The next action that was taken by the king was to throw the men and their entire families into the lion's den who had devised this decree as a trick to get rid of Daniel. The lions devoured the evil people. The angel was there as a protector for Daniel, who was a faithful follower. People may try to find fault in a believer and sometimes become jealous, but God sees the truth in a heart that follows His commands. The action of protection from the angel was God's whispered message to Daniel.

The Angel's Message to Mary

Mary was just a young teenage girl when she was chosen by Joseph to become his wife. Mary and Joseph were both faithful followers of the Lord. They both did right in the eyes of the Lord and God favored Mary. What happened to her next is written in the scriptures that most of us have read during the Christmas season. My pastor husband has often said to imagine the circumstances that were happening and to place yourself in the picture. An Angel Gabriel appeared before Mary to give her a message from God. I am sure she was frightened, but she submitted to listening carefully to the words that were being spoken to her at this chosen time in her life.

Luke 1:26-38, Now in the sixth month the angel Gabriel was sent by God to a city of Galilee named Nazareth, to a virgin betrothed to a man whose name was Joseph, of the house of David. The virgin's name was Mary. And having come in, the angel said to her, "Rejoice, highly favored one, the Lord is with you; blessed are you among women!" But when she saw him, she was troubled at his saying, and considered what manner of greeting this was. Then the angel said to her, "Do not be afraid, Mary, for you have found favor with God. And behold, you will conceive in your womb and bring forth a Son, and shall call His name Jesus. He will be great, and will be called the Son of the Highest; and the Lord God will give Him the throne of His father David. And He will reign over the house of Jacob forever, and of His kingdom there will be no end." Then Mary said to the angel, "How can this be, since I do not know a man?" And the angel answered and said to her, "The Holy Spirit will come upon you, and the power of the Highest will overshadow you; therefore, also, that Holy One who is to be born will be called the Son of God. Now indeed, Elizabeth your relative has also conceived a son in her old age; and this is now the sixth month for her who was called barren. For with God nothing will be impossible." Then Mary said, "Behold the maidservant of the Lord! Let it be to me according to your word." And the angel departed from her. NKJV

Elizabeth was Mary's cousin, and she had just conceived. The scriptures began "In the sixth month", and this was the time in Elizabeth's pregnancy. Now, this is the first time that an angel had a name that presented the message. He greeted her first saying she had been highly favored and that the Lord was with her. The message that she would be with child disturbed her because she was a virgin. She was to become the mother of the final King of Israel and He will be son of the Most High. His Kingdom will never end, and the promise made to King David will be finally fulfilled! This was a glorious whispered message that has blessed us all as believers. He chose an angel to bring this whispered message to a favored young girl at just the right time in the history of humanity. God would become a man and dwell with the people. Nothing is impossible with God.

I began to pray after writing the scriptures and stories of the four previous encounters that people had with angels when God revealed something to me that I feel should be shared. First, God sent angels to bring a message from Him and the angels are not to be worshiped. God will speak through the power of the Holy Spirit, but angels are sent to give messages when needed. The message needed is to bring understanding to the person and to give them strength during a hardship they may have to face. Can you imagine what Mary would have done if she had found out that she was pregnant and did not know how it happened? Could you imagine what Joseph would have done if an angel had not appeared to him in a dream? Mary would have been stoned and we would not have a living Savior today! Please, be careful that God alone is worshiped!

An Angel Rescues Peter

Peter had become very bold in witnessing for the Lord after the death and resurrection of the Lord Jesus Christ. He would get himself in trouble with the law of the land several times for preaching salvation that comes through faith in Jesus. The experience at Pentecost filled believers with the wisdom and power from on high. Peter became a proactive and powerful preacher after the Holy Spirit filled him to overflowing. Can you imagine preaching the truth of Jesus and having thousands of people accept Jesus Christ as their Savior? The new church had a powerful beginning. King Herod had arrested several of the people who belonged to this church and it was at this time that James, the brother of John, was slain by the sword. King Herod went looking for Peter because this seemed to be what the Jews wanted. Peter was found and arrested. He was placed in jail with several guards watching over him. This time was during the Passover time, so the trial would not take place until after the traditional feast. The church began to pray for Peter's protection and release from jail.

> *Acts 12:5-11 So Peter was kept in prison, but the church was earnestly praying to God for him. The night before Herod was to bring him to trial, Peter was sleeping between two soldiers, bound with two chains, and sentries stood guard at the entrance. Suddenly an angel of the Lord appeared and a light shone in the cell. He struck Peter on the side and woke him up. "Quick, get up!" he said, and the chains fell off Peter's wrists. Then the angel said to him, "Put on your clothes and sandals." And Peter did so. "Wrap your cloak around you and follow me," the angel told him. Peter followed him out of the prison, but he had no idea that what the angel was doing was really happening; he thought he was seeing a vision. They passed the first and second guards and came to the iron gate leading to the city. It opened for them by itself,*

and they went through it. When they had walked the length of one street, suddenly the angel left him. Then Peter came to himself and said, "Now I know without a doubt that the Lord sent his angel and rescued me from Herod's clutches and from everything the Jewish people were anticipating." NIV

Can you imagine what it may have been like to be chained to a rock wall in a dark cell and then a bright light fills the room? Our family lived in Italy for a couple of years and toured the jails that were common during the time that Peter was living, and they were very dark. Some of them were underground and rock walls. The jails were definitely not barred with private facilities for the prisoners. They were dungeons and dark! Peter was chained to the walls of the dungeon when the angel awakened him. The chains just fell off his wrists, and he walked out of the jail. He was not clothed either, so the angel told him to put his clothes and sandals on so that he could walk outside. Peter did think he was dreaming, but once the angel had left, he knew what he had experienced was not a dream. He had had an encounter with an angel who had given him a message from God. He immediately left to go where the church had been praying for him. The young lady who answered the door thought it was Peter's ghost at first and then realized that it was actually Peter. Their prayers had been answered, and God sent an angel to rescue Peter from the hands of King Herod. The angel provided safety for Peter at the request of a praying church. A church that prays together will receive answered prayer and hear God's whispers.

An Angel Whispers to Philip

The persecution of the church broke out in Jerusalem, and Stephen has just been stoned because of his witness against them for being stiff-necked people who had crucified Jesus Christ. He stated that they would find ways to resist the Holy Spirit, so this aroused the people's anger that ended up with Stephen being stoned. Saul witnessed this stoning after giving his approval and arrested many of the believers. He was determined to stop this new church from growing. The disciples were now scattered through Judea and Samaria. Philip was in a city in Samaria proclaiming Christ, and the people witnessed miracles. Many were healed from demon possessions and healed from their illnesses. Great joy broke out because the people believed, were healed and witnessed the power of the Holy Spirit. There was a man named Simon who practiced sorcery who had seemed to have great powers. The people of Samaria followed him because of the magic that he performed, but then he heard the message from Philip. Simon was transformed into a believer and was baptized. Peter and John soon arrived seeing the multitudes that were willing to accept fully the power of the Holy Spirit. Just believing was not enough. You must pray personally to accept Jesus Christ as your Savior, and then you will receive the indwelling power of the Holy Spirit.

Philip continued proclaiming Jesus Christ when an angel of the Lord gave him direct instructions from the Lord.

> *Acts 8:26-40 Now an angel of the Lord spoke to Philip, saying, "Arise and go toward the south along the road which goes down from Jerusalem to Gaza." This is desert. So he arose and went. And behold, a man of Ethiopia, a eunuch of great authority under Candace the queen of the Ethiopians, who had charge of all her treasury, and had come to Jerusalem to worship, was returning. And sitting in his chariot, he was reading Isaiah the prophet. Then the Spirit said to Philip, "Go near and overtake this chariot." So Philip ran to him, and heard him reading the prophet Isaiah, and said, "Do you understand what you are reading?" And he said, "How can I, unless someone guides me?" And he asked Philip to come up and sit with him. The place in the Scripture which he read was this: "He was led as a sheep to the slaughter; And as a lamb before its shearer is silent, So He opened not His mouth. In His humiliation His justice was taken away, And who will declare His generation? For His life is taken from the earth." So the eunuch answered Philip and said, "I ask you, of whom does the prophet say this, of himself or of some other man?" Then Philip opened his mouth, and beginning at this Scripture, preached Jesus to him. Now as they went down the road, they came to some water. And the eunuch said, "See,*

here is water. What hinders me from being baptized?" Then Philip said, "If you believe with all your heart, you may." And he answered and said, "I believe that Jesus Christ is the Son of God." So he commanded the chariot to stand still. And both Philip and the eunuch went down into the water, and he baptized him. Now when they came up out of the water, the Spirit of the Lord caught Philip away, so that the eunuch saw him no more; and he went on his way rejoicing. But Philip was found at Azotus. And passing through, he preached in all the cities till he came to Caesarea. NKJV

Did you notice that an angel whispered instructions to Philip where to go next, and then the Holy Spirit whispered to him to go stand by the chariot when he saw the Ethiopian eunuch? There was urgency to the message that Philip understood where he was to go next, and that is why God sent the angel. God chooses the need for a message from an angel because He sees the future and knows that there is a need to know without any doubt that God is there to give His strength. Hagar, Daniel, Balaam from the Old Testament and Mary, Joseph, Peter and Philip from the New Testament received messages from God through angels. These messages strengthened their faith in the powerful Creator. Every person was made stronger in what he had to face in his experiences because an angel had touched him. The whispers that come from angels are real, but it is never meant to replace the power and presence of the Holy Spirit in a believer's life.

Do Angels whisper today?

The telephone rang at 9:00 p.m. on a Sunday evening. Our family had just gotten home from church, and the children were being put to bed. My husband said that my sister was on the telephone from Phoenix, Arizona. She began to share that our mother was not released from the hospital, as planned, that morning, but was placed in the Intensive Care Unit instead. She had experienced severe abdominal pain and walked to the nurse's station because they did not respond to her call button. The nurse began to check her out and called the doctor right away. She had a large blood clot just under her skin covering her entire abdomen. My pastor brother got on the telephone and asked that I take the earliest flight to Phoenix. Mom may not live through the night. My emotions were running high when I got off the phone. With the assistance from several members of the church family I was on the midnight flight to Phoenix from Anchorage, Alaska. The flight would take ten hours.

The flight made two stops. One in San Francisco and one in Los Angles, California, before landing in Phoenix. The flight from Los Angles to Phoenix was only one hour, but I was getting tired. My husband and children remained in Alaska. The aisle seat was comfortable, and I was settled ready for the plane to make the last leg of this trip. I watched many people coming onto the plane, but one other passenger drew my interest. He was shaking hands with an older gentleman saying good-bye. The older gentleman left the plane. That seemed odd because most people say their good-byes before they get on to the plane. I shrugged my shoulders and never thought anymore about what I had just witnessed. We were all fastened in, and the plane began it's ascent. The young man that I had been watching turned around and began looking at me. He continued watching me the entire flight. I began to get uneasy and would not look into his eyes. When the plane landed, I prepared, very quickly, to get off the plane. I rushed passed the young man but decided to look back at him. Our eyes met! His look stripped my soul naked, he knew me, and then he said **"God is with you"**. I looked back again and he was gone.

The next two weeks were difficult, but the presence of the Lord gave me a peace that I had never experienced in my life. My mother lived another three weeks before she went to be with the Lord. There were people whom I met during this difficult time that became blessings to me and me to them.

Hebrews 1:14 "Are not all angels ministering spirits sent to serve those who will inherit salvation?" NIV

1. *Pray:*

   Lord, I believe that angels do exist. I know that it is your choice to work through when the need is there to reveal your message. I have learned, in the Scripture, how you have given messages through angels.

2. *Reflection:*

   What have you learned about angels? Do you believe that God could choose an angel to give you a message? Why or why not?

CHAPTER 10

The Whisper When Witnessing

Y
ou have been introduced to God's whispers in nature, through prayer, through God's plan, through music and through angels as we studied the scriptures together. Keep focusing on the whispers of God when you become obedient to witnessing. When a person begins to share his faith there are several ways this can be done. There is a term called life style witnessing. This is living out your faith in your actions and attitude before people you come into contact daily. You and I need to be reminded that, as believers, God is still working on our hearts as you read your Bible and pray. The best way to be a witness is to allow the Holy Spirit to have His way in your hearts and a desire to act when He prompts us. Your testimony is a powerful tool.

You probably are saying to yourself that you are frightened to speak out and witness. You are afraid of rejection more than anything, but it is worth the possibility of rejection to experience someone coming to know the Lord. This will bring eternal security to the person you are witnessing to if he or she opens their heart to what you are sharing.

There was a precious senior lady that was in a Bible Study I once facilitated that shared that she had never witnessed to anyone her entire life, and she wanted to know how to begin? She was concerned about a young man who was dying of cancer, and he did not have much time to live. I stopped the scheduled Bible study and worked through a track called "Eternal Life" with the entire ladies' class. That Sunday evening she came running up to me with excitement stating that she did what we did in class, and the man had accepted Jesus Christ as his Savior. She was absolutely glowing! She told me that she asked him if they could go somewhere private because she had something she wanted to share with him. He agreed and while she read the tract to him page by page, he opened his heart to accepting Jesus. He cried and thanked her for caring enough about him to share this truth. He died soon after he had prayed to accept Jesus as His Savior. Do not be afraid. The Holy Spirit will whisper the right words for you to speak.

> *Ephesians 2:10," For we are God's workmanship, created in Christ Jesus to do good works, which God prepared in advance for us to do." NIV*

The Witness through Peter at Pentecost

Peter was reactive and many times spoke before he would listen to what was being said. He was the disciple who denied Jesus three times before the cock crowed as told to him by Jesus. Yet, just prior in the Garden of Gethsemane he drew a sword and cut off an ear of one of the guards that came to arrest Jesus. He was just a little bit erratic in his personality. How could he possibly be a positive witness for the Lord?

Shortly after Jesus was crucified, Peter was out fishing again with some of the other disciples. Peter saw on the shoreline a man asking them if they had caught any fish yet. Jesus said to cast their nets on the right side of the boat. They did what he said and then could not haul the net in because of the weight of all the fish that were caught. The Bible tells us the disciple that Jesus loved recognized that it was Jesus on the shoreline. They yelled out, "It is the Lord"! Peter then wrapped his outer garment around his waist and jumped into the water to swim to Jesus. How impulsive is that for a grown man to do? The disciples ate some fish that were prepared by Jesus on an open fire shortly after everyone came to shore. The conversation that followed between Jesus and Peter was very interesting. Peter just did not seem to understand the questions that Jesus kept asking him. (John 21:15-19)

Scholars have described that Jesus was asking Peter if he had the same kind of love that Jesus had for him. Jesus saw his heart when Peter was actually saying that he loved him like a friend. He wanted Peter to respond with a God like love for Jesus so that he would eventually have a heart to love and care for his people. He wanted Peter to be willing to die for the sake of sharing the Gospel of Jesus Christ. Peter did not understand what was being said because he became discouraged at the continued question of whether he loved Jesus. Jesus wanted Peter to share with the people the truth of who He was and could become in their life.

In the days that followed, Peter would be in an upper room in a home of a friend with many disciples waiting for the promised Holy Spirit to come upon them. There was a sudden rush of violent like wind and what looked like tongues of fire that rested on everyone. (Acts: 2:1-4) The crowd outside heard the disruption and became confused and bewildered after they had heard these disciples speaking in their own languages. The people surrounded them saying that they must be drunk. Then here comes Peter again, but this time he was a bold witness of what had just happened. He began to speak to the people.

> *Acts 2:14-21, Then Peter stood up with the Eleven, raised his voice and addressed the crowd: "Fellow Jews and all of you who live in Jerusalem, let me explain this to you; listen carefully to what I say. These men are not drunk, as you suppose. It's only nine in the morning! No, this is what was spoken by the Prophet Joel: "In the last days, God says, I will pour out my Spirit on all people. Your sons and daughters will prophesy, your young men will see visions, your old men will dream dreams. Even on my servants, both men and women, I will pour out my Spirit in those days, and they will prophesy. I will show wonders in the heaven above and signs on the earth below, blood and fire and billows of smoke. The sun will be turned to darkness and the moon to blood before the coming of the great and glorious day of the Lord. And*

everyone who calls on the name of the Lord will be saved.'
NIV

Peter continued his witness by stating that Jesus whom they had crucified is both Lord and Christ. The power and the whispers of the Holy Spirit penetrated the hearts and about three thousand people accepted the Lord Jesus as their personal Lord and Savior. We have the same power of the Holy Spirit living in us as believers today, but have we lost our boldness? He asked us to be available, and the Holy Spirit will whisper the right words as we witness. Who will be our next Peter, or someone who will help transform a world that will bring the light of Jesus Christ to people who need to hear this truth today?

The Witness to Saul that would change the Gentile World

Saul was a prominent man in history who, as stated, had been circumcised on the 8th day according the Jewish custom. He was from the tribe of Benjamin; he was zealous regarding the Laws of Moses. He was a Pharisee, and he was active in persecuting the new church. He was somebody who people took notice of when seeing him due to his assertive personality. He seemed to have been very self-righteous and was extremely educated. He truly felt he had all the right answers for everything. He had several believers in Jesus Christ arrested. He actually would drag people from their homes if he heard that they were believers. You definitely would not want him against you for fear of what he could do to you. We sometimes live in fear because of people who seemed to share a personality like he did. How do you witness to a person who has total disrespect for your belief in Jesus Christ? Well, let us see how Saul became Paul and ended up writing most of the New Testament.

Saul had gone to the High Priest asking for letters to the synagogues in Damascus so that he could find the people who belonged to the Way (the new believers). He headed for Damascus when something happened that would change his life.

Acts 9:3-9, As he neared Damascus on his journey, suddenly
a light from heaven flashed around him. He fell to the ground

and heard a voice say to him, "Saul, Saul, why do you persecute me?" "Who are you, Lord?" Saul asked. "I am Jesus, whom you are persecuting," he replied. "Now get up and go into the city, and you will be told what you must do." The men traveling with Saul stood there speechless; they heard the sound but did not see anyone. Saul got up from the ground, but when he opened his eyes he could see nothing. So they led him by the hand into Damascus. For three days he was blind, and did not eat or drink anything. NIV

Jesus whispered words to Saul that only he could hear, and the sudden light caught his attention. Saul became blind from this experience. He was spiritually blind before he had this experience to the truth of Jesus Christ, and now he had was physically blind.

The next event that happened was the whisper to a disciple named Ananias who Jesus called to in a vision. He was told to go to a man to restore his sight and gave him exact directions. He prayed to the Lord saying that this man was destroying new believers and was afraid to obey the request. He told Ananias that Saul was now a chosen instrument to carry His name to Kings, Gentiles and to the people of Israel. He was going to suffer much for the sake of Jesus Christ.

Ananias followed the Lord's commands and went to Saul placing his hands on him to heal him. Ananias told Saul what had happened to him because the Lord had revealed the experience in detail to him. Saul was healed from his temporary blindness and was fed some food to regain his strength. He immediately began to preach the truth of Jesus Christ in the synagogues. The people were surprised at the changes in Saul's life, but when you encounter the living God, you are transformed into a new person. What used to be important to him did not matter anymore. The power of the whispered words from Jesus Christ is the only action that could have changed a heart like the zealous Saul. I would call it shock therapy!

His letters that he would eventually be transcribed would change a waiting world that was not of the Jewish faith. Many Jewish people were saved at the words, actions and preaching that came from Saul. His zealous and proactive nature of his personality was now motivated by the power of the Holy Spirit of God. He has become one of the most powerful witnesses that we have through the scriptures today.

When People Ask the Right Question

You were encouraged earlier that there can be life style witnessing, but you must keep yourself reading the word of God and staying close to the living Savior through prayer. You will slip in life style witnessing if you do not discipline yourself to spend time with the Lord daily. Our natural physical person is sinful. Life Style is a wonderful way to witness, but you must be prepared to share your witness verbally when a person asks you about the hope that lives in you. My pastor husband says lifestyle witnessing in not enough to win a person to the Lord. Lifestyle witnessing alone can sometimes give you an "I do not care attitude" about another person's soul. Jesus asked Peter if he loved Him. Do you love Jesus? You may say, "Yes, He is my best friend!" Do you love Jesus? You again may say, "Yes, like a brother!" Do you love Jesus? You may finally say, "Yes, I will obey and go the extra mile to tell others about Him, because I have learned to love others as Jesus loves them!" This is called "Agape Love". Agape is a god-like love that you grow to understand as you allow the Holy Spirit to work through your life.

People will start to ask questions when you are open to what the Holy Spirit wants to do through your life. People are seeking answers to the meaning of life, to not wanting to be alone, to stop making mistakes that hurt themselves and others. Jesus fills the gap for the personal needs we have to live in peace. People worry, they are afraid, they are confused, they have addictive habits, they have past hurtful experiences, they have self worth struggles and the list goes on and on. Do you love Jesus?

A person may come up to you and ask you "Are you a Christian?" What would your answer be? What if someone asked you to pray for him? Would you pray for that person on the spot? A person may ask you, "Why are you the way you are?" What would your answer be to him? What if someone asked to show them how to be saved and what does it mean? Do you know that this may be a whisper for you to respond?

When my husband and several men were attending seminary, there were two of us wives who were able to get a job in the same insurance company. We did the data processing at inputting new policies. Our boss was young and a proactive person. She would often talk to us about why our husbands were attending seminary and what did that mean? How long would we be able to work? She would ask why we were the way we were? She said that she truly wanted to know! She called us in her office and asked if we could go to lunch with her the next day? We agreed.

That evening the other woman and I met together to decide what to do. She had never witnessed, so I asked her to pray silently while I shared the truth about Jesus Christ during our luncheon the next day. The plan was set, but we needed to be sensitive to the prompting of the Holy Spirit from the other woman.

The luncheon was on, and we left the office together the next day. We enjoyed our lunch and the conversation was light. Then she asked, "What does it mean to be saved?" The door was opened by the whisper from God. By the time the luncheon was over she had prayed asking Jesus Christ to forgive her sins and to come into her heart! She became excited and felt at peace. She asked, "Why was this so easy to accept?" We told her that it was the Lord prompting her heart to accept what we shared. The Holy Spirit is the only power that will change a heart.

Another experience of when someone asked the right question was while I was at work in a medical clinic. I was a financial counselor and had a private office where a patient could speak to me without being overheard. My heart struggled working at this clinic and being asked to do this was very difficult. This young lady was making financial arrangements to get an abortion. She did not have the money, so I advised her about her options when the Lord asked me, "Invite her to your home!" I was quiet for a moment, and then I heard the request again in my heart. I finally asked what the Holy Spirit told me to ask. She then asked me, "Why would you be willing to do that for me?" I told her that it was not my idea, but the Holy Spirit of God asked me to ask her! She began to cry saying that she had asked God to forgive her and to please let her know that what she was attempting to do was wrong? She then said that she would not have the abortion and that she was calling her parents after leaving the clinic. The

Holy Spirit whispered His forgiveness to this young lady's heart that day. God placed me at the right place for the right reason.

Initiating Spiritual Conversations

We will talk about the weather to people without any stress in our conversations. We will talk about our children and our grandchildren with no effort, but what about bringing up a spiritual conversation? What is a spiritual conversation? Let me give you an example of what I am talking about. When you talk about the weather, you could ask "Did you see that beautiful sunrise that the Lord created for us to see this morning?" How hard would that be when talking about the weather?

In Oklahoma the wheat farmers are always concerned about having a good crop every year. I mentioned once to a farmer that I was praying for an abundant harvest for them as well as God reaping a spiritual harvest. He looked at me surprised at what I had said. Was this a spiritual conversation? People may continue the conversation once it has been started, but the subject may be dropped. My advice to you is to allow the Holy Spirit to open a person's heart. People will come back sometimes to continue a deeper conversation about the Lord with you, because you surrendered to opening a door. This is a no pressure way of witnessing that anybody could do.

I was working at a large hospital in Las Vegas, Nevada, where a co-worker of mine was assigned to train me when I first became employed. She was assertive with her training and was sometimes impatient, but I was a new employee. She started sharing with me something that was disturbing her in her personal life, and I told her that I would pray for her. This made her angry, and she did not want me working around her at all. She became more and more impatient with me. She eventually asked me why I did not get upset with her. To tell you the truth, I never knew that she was being rude.

The young lady had made several mistakes in her life that she was not proud of, and the expression of faith that she witnessed through me made her very uncomfortable. She finally opened up to me in time what all she had done.

Her brother was a strong believer in Jesus Christ and had an almost fatal automobile accident. He was in recovery for many years but maintained the memory of being a believer in Jesus Christ. She was angry with God for allowing this accident to happen to her brother. He would always tell her that he would be praying for her. Now, do you understand why she got mad at what I had said? One day she asked me to meet her in the Chapel at the hospital where we were working. She sat down next to me in the Chapel asking me how she could accept Jesus Christ as her Savior? Yes, she came back to me later because I was willing to have a spiritual conversation with her. She accepted Jesus Christ as her personal Savior and became a transformed believer!

One day she tapped me on the shoulder asking me if I would lead a few employees in prayer for another co-worker who was in critical condition at the hospital. She had asked our Supervisor for permission to ask me to do this and was told that it would be all right as long as we went outside the building. I got up from my chair and walked outside the building with 30 of the 50 employees following me. There were several other believers in my workplace who prayed that day. This was opportunity for us to unite together in prayer. Making the decision to have a spiritual conversation with a co-worker is what God used to guide this journey. He again only asks us to be available and He will whisper His words in our hearts.

1 Corinthians 2:10-16, "but God has revealed it to us by his Spirit. The Spirit searches all things, even the deep things of God. For who among men knows the thoughts of a man except the man's spirit within him? In the same way no one knows the thoughts of God except the Spirit of God. We have not received the spirit of the world but the Spirit who is from God, that we may understand what God has freely given us. This is what we speak, not in words taught us by human wisdom but in words taught by the Spirit, expressing spiritual truths in spiritual words. The man without the Spirit does not accept the things that come from the Spirit of God, for they are foolishness to him, and he cannot understand them, because they are spiritually discerned. The spiritual man makes judgments about all things, but he himself is

> *not subject to any man's judgment: For who has known the*
> *mind of the Lord that he may instruct him?' But we have the*
> *mind of Christ." NIV*

We need to be reminded that it is the wisdom and whispers of the Holy Spirit through a surrendered life in Jesus Christ that will give us the mind of Christ that will touch people's heart when witnessing.

Witnessing as the Body of Christ

The church is the body of Jesus Christ, and each member has been given a spiritual gift that gives strength to the body. We were meant to be interdependent with each other as believers. We need to be reminded that each individual member of the body needs to make every effort on his own to grow deeper in his relationship with the Lord, but studying and being with other believers helps us to grow. The Bible tells us to not forsake meeting with other believers. There is power and strength that is generated from the prayers of others. The power of prayers from people being together all night is what led Peter from jail. The angel responded to the prayers that came from the church that was gathered together in prayer. The wisdom that comes from a gifted saint brings light to a scripture that you may not have understood. We are all at different levels of growth in our relationships with Jesus, so we need each other.

Here is another nature lesson for a moment just to share a few things. Animals often gather together in herds like the deer, the antelope, the buffalo, and the zebra. There was a documentary being filmed on the wilder beast in Africa one time that showed the herd drinking at a river basin and then all of a sudden a crocodile grabbed one of their young. The herd gathered immediately around the baby attacking the crocodile until the little wilder beast was released from the jaws. The herd was not concerned for their individual safety but the safety of the one being attacked. We are not called herds, but the purpose of us gathering together is to protect each other from an enemy that is of greater threat to the individual that could destroy the entire body. The church body is called on by God to protect the individual believer through prayer, fellowship, encouragement, witnessing and the teaching God's truth.

We have an enemy, and his name is destruction. He lies to the hearts of believers and to a body of believers. He causes confusion and disruption. There is very little peace that is experienced when he is at work. We must learn to recognize that the enemy is Satan and that he does not want the Kingdom of God to grow. Let us gather around each member of the body of church that may be attacked by this enemy. No one is exempt, not even a pastor. We sometimes may think God is disciplining us, and that may be true, but Jesus said to count it all joy when we are experiencing difficulties through serving the Lord.

> *Romans 5:1-5 "Therefore, since we have been justified through faith, we have peace with God through our Lord Jesus Christ, through whom we have gained access by faith into this grace in which we now stand. And we rejoice in the hope of the glory of God. Not only so, but we also rejoice in our sufferings, because we know that suffering produces perseverance; perseverance, character; and character, hope. And hope does not disappoint us, because God has poured out his love into our hearts by the Holy Spirit, whom he has given us." NIV*

When does God whisper to a group that is serving the Lord? Any believer in the group can speak the whisper that comes from God. In a Bible study with a group of women, in a private home, we were studying the Book of Philemon. The letter was written to Philemon from Paul regarding his slave Onesimus, who had run away from him. Onesimus had been in jail with Paul and had become a believer in Jesus Christ. Paul asked Philemon to forgive and accept this slave back to his care because he was now a fellow believer.

This book is not very long and it would only take a few minutes to read. The question was finally asked by one on the ladies, "What happened to Onesimus? Was he forgiven?" The book does not directly answer this question. There was an uncomfortable amount of silent, when someone heard the whisper in their heart saying, "You have the letter as proof that this request was honored; otherwise the letter would have been destroyed."

We can witness the whispers of God as believers in the body of Jesus Christ through any member. We are mandated to lift each other up and to love one another as we learn to love the Lord. Do we love Jesus? When we learn to love Jesus, we learn to love what He loves!

Be Prepared for a Divine Appointment

We meet people every day as we live our life. Sometimes we choose not to leave our homes, so interaction with others is not always possible. When we have jobs we are with people. We go to the grocery stores, the post office, and we drive our automobiles and speak with people on the telephone. Unless we are hermits, we encounter people in all walks of life. There are several reality shows on television these days, so we watch people! We are not alone in this vast world, so what is the plan of God when he created so many human beings? He wants people to know that they are sinners but could be forgiven. He wants people who feel alone to not be lonely anymore. He wants people who feel they are not accepted to know they are accepted. He wants people who think there is no God to know that there is a God and a Savior. He wants people who think there is not life after death to know that God promises eternal life with Him. He wants people who have experienced abuse to know they are loved. Do we love Jesus? Do we hear His whispers when the asked us to be His witnesses?

While working in a hospital business office a social worker walked through the office asking if anyone had an extra bedroom in her home for a mother and a newborn. She was a minor and could not go back to her parent's home. There was a special fund that was going to pay for her hospital stay, but she needed to be released to another home.

God had provided a large home for us to live in, and we did have an extra bedroom. My husband and I decided to allow her to come to our home. The Holy Spirit, in a gentle whisper, prompted this action. She told me that she needed to know that day and promised that the stay would only be for a few days. Our family agreed that this is what we called a divine appointment before even meeting this young girl.

The social worker, my husband and I walked to the girl's room to meet her and her mother. My heart cried to the Lord in thanksgiving for giving us a chance to love this scared timid young teenage girl. The baby boy was still quite small lying in the hospital bassinet. Her mother arrived with a several questions about our home and who lived in the home. We told her everything she needed to know that seemed to satisfy the concerns that she may have had. There was one question that became the right question and that was, "Why are you doing this?" The answer was that the Lord wanted us to do this for her daughter and that we did not want anything from her or her family. This young lady ended up living with us for about six months. She turned eighteen years old during this time and accepted Jesus Christ as her Savior. She met a young man at our church whom she married. Be willing to be obedient to a divine appointment that the Lord may put in your path to share the truth of who Jesus could be in that person's life. The whisper that comes from the Lord may end up blessing you.

> *Romans 12:9-16 "Love must be sincere. Hate what is evil; cling to what is good. Be devoted to one another in brotherly love. Honor one another above yourselves. Never be lacking in zeal, but keep your spiritual fervor, serving the Lord. Be joyful in hope, patient in affliction, faithful in prayer. Share with God's people who are in need. Practice hospitality. Bless those who persecute you; bless and do not curse. Rejoice with those who rejoice; mourn with those who mourn. Live in harmony with one another. Do not be proud, but be willing to associate with people of low position. Do not be conceited." NIV*

We must be surrendered to the hearing the whisper that comes from God regarding a divine appointment for you to accept.

Being Genuine when Witnessing

The Lord has asked us to put on the full armor of God as found in Ephesians 6:13-18. The mandate to witness is part of putting on the full armor of God. As you share the Gospel of Jesus Christ, it should be genuine and not pushy. Try to walk the walk and not just talk the talk. Children and teenagers are very perceptive when a person is not real with them. Living in a relationship with the Lord by reading His Word and spending time in prayer will develop in you a desire to be more like Jesus. People are drawn to genuine love and concern for their well-being. Children are more ready to receive the love of the Lord through a whispered witness than most adults are due to not having as many negative experiences. I pray that people would all be receptive like they seem to be, but it is not always possible. Adults still respond to genuine love and concern, so be real with people. Spend time in prayer for those who are lost asking God to send you someone that needs to hear His whispered message of Salvation. Do you love Jesus?

> *Acts 1:8, But you will receive power when the Holy Spirit comes on you; and you will be my witnesses in Jerusalem, and in all Judea and Samaria, and to the ends of the earth." NIV*

1. *Pray:*

    Lord, I want to be a positive witness to help to share the truth to other people. I know that I cannot speak clearly without the power of the Holy Spirit whispering through my life. I pray that you draw people to me that need to receive Jesus Christ as their Savior and give me the right words that will make your message easily understood.

2. *Reflection:*

    What ways has the Holy Spirit shown you how to witness? Do you have a desire for others to come to the knowledge of the saving faith in Jesus Christ?

CHAPTER 11

The Whisper of Mercy

L et us take another fictional journey together. You and your mate received a large inheritance. You wanted a home of your own, so you went looking in the area that you wanted to live. The choices were numerous, but you found one that would make you comfortable for many years. You bought the home and began to decorate it with furniture, wall coverings and had a swimming pool built for relaxation. You were living the American dream. You noticed that people were coming to your doorstep introducing themselves as your new neighbors. One particular couple came quite frequently. You begin to notice that small items were beginning to disappear from your china cabinet, from the fireplace mantle and from the kitchen. You decided to put hidden cameras all through your home. This couple came for dinner one night, and then you noticed one would get up and leave. This happened several times. You later viewed the cameras and noticed that one or the other was in your bedroom or the kitchen or in the living room putting things in their pockets. You both ask each other how to approach this problem?

You and your mate called this couple to ask if you could come to their home. NO! They answered so abruptly. They said that they could come to your home. You said, "Maybe another time, but not today". The next day you noticed the wife of the other couple walking down a street with a bag of groceries, so you followed her to her home. The home was in a rundown neighborhood. The door in the front was hanging off its hinges, and the yard was trashed with dirty bags, torn up children's toys and auto parts everywhere. You look at each other wondering if they had children because they said they did not have any children. You came every day for about one week observing this home, and there did not seem to be any children playing. Finally you had seen enough, so you decided to call them to come over for dinner.

You prayed asking God to give you wisdom on how to approach what you had seen? The conversation begins with you asking them questions about their professions, how many rooms did they have in their home and if they had a swimming pool? The tears begin to flow down the woman's face. Her husband keeps quiet. She starts to tell you the truth about their living conditions, and they did have a little boy. She cried telling you that their son had died when he was ten years old. They both finally admitted that they were stealing from you so they could buy food. The woman said that her husband's unemployment check only paid the mortgage payment. They apologized for the wrong that was done and would immediately return the items that they had at their home. They had only pawned one of the items. The women told you where the pawnshop was in hopes of getting the item back.

Her husband had been looking for a job but could not find one. They pawned the item they took for cash to buy groceries. The woman asked, "What are you going to do?" "Are you going to call the police?" You had their confessions and the videotapes. Are you going to give them money? Would they keep coming back for more money? Are you going help find the man a job? What would the mercy of Jesus Christ do in this situation? You have to decide to do what is best. What will be your decision? You may want to remember what is whispered in the Scriptures regarding mercy. This couple chose to forgive and guide them to help to better their lives.

Love the Lord

> *Luke 10:27-28, He answered: "Love the Lord your God with all your heart and with all your soul and with all your strength and with all your mind'; and, 'Love your neighbor as*

yourself.'" "You have answered correctly," Jesus replied. "Do this and you will live." NIV

Jesus was having a conversation with an expert in the law when the expert said the greatest commandment was to love the Lord with all your soul, strength and mind. It is a law, but do people follow this law? The law is very strict, and it is almost impossible to follow everything that is written, so some of the experts seem to make up their own interpretation. This is true today as people read the Scriptures. You cannot understand the true meaning of any Scripture with out the prompting of the Holy Spirit. Prayer opens the door to God's wisdom. When you start down the path to love the Lord, the way the law says, you gain a deeper understanding to the heart of God. Can you really love someone with all of your heart? Can you really love someone with all of your soul? Can you really love someone with your entire mind? God desires you to be totally committed to Him with all of who you are and could be, in humility. What benefit would you receive if you were to humanly be able to surrender to this kind of love? You must believe in Jesus Christ and then accept that you are loved. You surrender, with a child like faith, to God's love. His love is pure and Holy. The Lord's love for you is not physical but spiritual. He will reach your mind and your soul. Can you love someone without first meeting him or her and getting to know them? How do you get acquainted with someone without speaking to them or allowing them to speak to you? You should be silent and listen for the sweet whispers that will gently penetrate your heart with understanding. Jesus did reply and said, "Do this and you will live."

Picture yourself sitting at the feet of Jesus listening to this conversation. You are a new believer and are hungry to learn the truth of the law that was just mentioned. You ask yourself, "Can I learn to love the Lord God with all my soul and all my strength and all of my mind?" Do you love Him now like that? Remember you are just a new believer. Please be honest about this question. If your answer is, "Not yet", then keep reading and listening to the whispers that will be prompting your heart. The Holy Spirit will reveal the love that God always had for you. The Scriptures tell us that we love God because He first loved us. *(1 John 4:19, We love because he first loved us. NIV)*

We are not only to love God, but we are to love other believers. You are to love your neighbors as you love yourself and as Jesus Christ loves you. You may be thinking about a neighbor you just had a fight with over the noise coming from his house late last night when you were trying to sleep. You had to get up early the next morning to go to work. You remember the yelling that took place and you feel guilt over the things that you said. You ask yourself, "Was what I did and said a positive witness reflecting my belief in Jesus Christ?" You need to make things right and apologize to your neighbor for your attitude. If he does not accept your apology, then you have to do what the Scriptures tell you to do, and then you pray for them. When you pray for somebody with whom you may be in conflict, it is very hard to continue to stay angry. Try asking God to bless them, and it will soften your heart. Getting even just brings you down to their level of disobedience. Jesus told you to love your neighbors as you love yourself.

Who is your Neighbor?

> *Luke 10:29, But he wanted to justify himself, so he asked Jesus, "And who is my neighbor?" NIV*

Who is your neighbor? Do you get along with him? Do you even know him? Are neighbors limited to just the people who live around you? What about the people at your church? What about the people who you work with on a day-to-day basis? What about the people who you greet in a grocery store? Who are you to love like you love yourself? Sometimes it truly is a difficult request of Jesus to ask you to love your neighbors like you love yourself! Neighbors can be difficult to love, at times.

We had a middle aged single woman living next door to us in a senior mobile home park, who had several cats. There were strays all over the park, so she began to feed them. The cats began to grow in number outside of her mobile home. The park asked that the animal control be called and to not feed the stray cats. We reported her to the manager at first, but nothing was done. We attempted to speak to her, but she would just slam the door saying that we were cat haters. One of the strays was pregnant, so she took it into her home to protect the kittens. She began to take several of them in her home but would let them out at night. They started lying on our front porch, so one night we grabbed one of them that was on our porch. My husband went to Wal-Mart and found a loving home for this cat. We told her the next day that we found a good home for one of the cats, and she got angry for taking the cat. She called the police and told him that we stole her cat. The police came over to thank us for getting rid of the cat. She called us names publicly and told everybody, who would listen to her, that my husband was a cat killer. She would come outside at 2:00 a.m., stand on her front porch that was next to our bedroom, and call out for the cat. This went on for two hours every night, and this lasted for about two weeks. We sent her a card apologizing for hurting her, but she would not accept our apology. Her twin sister lived on the other side of us and apologized for her sister's attitude. She actually encouraged us to find homes for the cats, if we could. We were concerned that some of these cats may have rabies. We did nothing to get even. Did we love her? Yes, we loved her and did not want her upset. Did we like her attitude? No, but that was her choice to stay angry. She was evicted because she broke the rules of the park. The other neighbors in the park turned her in for disturbing the peace. She was one neighbor who was difficult, but she did not do anything that could not be forgiven.

Yes, neighbors can be difficult to forgive and love. With the assistance that comes from the Holy Spirit we can love our neighbors. We need to show the mercy that God expects us to share with people who are not lovable. You may have had a friend or a family member who hurt you. They are your neighbors, too. What does the Scriptures tell you about having mercy for a wrong done to you? You need to realize that sometimes you are not so lovable and neither am I. What about a neighbor who may need help that we can give them?

Jesus Shares a Parable

> *Luke 10:30-36, In reply Jesus said: "A man was going down from Jerusalem to Jericho, when he fell into the hands of robbers. They stripped him of his clothes, beat him and went away, leaving him half dead. A priest happened to be going*

> *down the same road, and when he saw the man, he passed by*
> *on the other side. So too, a Levite, when he came to the place*
> *and saw him, passed by on the other side. But a Samaritan,*
> *as he traveled, came where the man was; and when he saw*
> *him, he took pity on him. He went to him and bandaged his*
> *wounds, pouring on oil and wine. Then he put the man on*
> *his own donkey, took him to an inn and took care of him.*
> *The next day he took out two silver coins and gave them to*
> *the innkeeper. 'Look after him,' he said, 'and when I return,*
> *I will reimburse you for any extra expense you may have.'*
> *"Which of these three do you think was a neighbor to the man*
> *who fell into the hands of robbers?" NIV*

You need to ask yourself who you would be in this picture. Have you seen people being attacked and did nothing? Have you seen a child being abused publicly and did nothing. Do people today want to get involved? Do people want to just protect their own safety and comfort? What about someone who needs a ride to the doctor? What about someone who needs to go grocery shopping and cannot drive? What about asking someone to live in your home that is homeless? What about giving a person some of your groceries, or buy a tank of gasoline, or care for their child(ren) while they go to work on a moments notice? Do you mind being interrupted to help someone when you have other plans? Have you made the choice to change your plans? Have you given your last dollar to someone who needed it more than you did? If you have saved a person's life, or stopped abuse of a child, then that is an act of mercy. When you reach out to care for others less fortunate than yourself, you are showing mercy the way that Jesus did for you. Jesus saw you when you were not so lovely, He saw you when you were hurting, and He saw you when you thought you could not be forgiven. Jesus knew what you could become under His grace.

Do you remember a time when you gave to someone expecting nothing in return? You knew that this person could never pay you back when you loaned them money to pay for a doctor's visit. How did it make you feel? Were you at peace and joyful that you followed the example Jesus Christ showed you or were you angry that you allowed yourself to be taken advantage of? There are people that tell you sad stories that are not genuine, but there are those that are real.

A sister in Christ shared a moment in her life that blessed her beyond her expectation. She said that she was working as a waitress and someone brought in a woman and two children to buy them a meal. The little boy, who was about six years old, prayed thanking God for the meal. He went on to ask God to protect his mommy and not let them lose their home. He continued by asking God for school supplies, because their mommy did not have the money. Then he said "Amen". This waitress did not actually hear the prayer, but another waitress did. The other waitress told my friend the story with tears rolling down her cheek. My friend talked with her boss and asked if there was something they could do? He walked up to the table and told everyone the meal was free. He knew the person who brought the women and her children in for the meal, so he asked where they lived? She gave her boss the address. My friend never spoke to this family, but right after work she drove to a dollar store to spend her tip money for school supplies for these children. The next day she prayed asking God to allow her to get large tips that night so that she could provide maybe some rent money. The Lord blessed and she then went to her boss asking him to deliver the school supplies and pay the rent? He did do just as she asked him to do. She did not want anybody to know what she had done for this precious family. Two weeks later the family came back for another meal and wanted to know who the waitress was who had been so very kind to them? She was found out. The little boy ran to her to thank her for the school supplies! She said that was the greatest payment she could have ever received. She is thankful to the whisper of the Holy Spirit that invited her to get involved in this act of mercy.

Have you avoided being a friend with someone that you thought may take up too much of your time? You may be a private person who has a difficult time getting acquainted with people. A private person may be just the right person do a special act of mercy without anybody knowing about it, which will bring glory to God, in his service to Him. We have an amazing God because He will work through all personalities. You should be thankful for how God has made you to be and how willing He is to include you in working with Him. I believe that the Bible tells us not to boast about what we have done for the Lord because we have already received our reward. What you do in secret will allow the opportunity for God to lift you up in the fullness of His time and give you His reward. You will be blessed.

The Reply to the Question

Luke 10:37, The expert in the law replied, "The one who had mercy on him." Jesus told him, "Go and do likewise." NIV

Wow! We are commanded to 'Go and do likewise! Can you reflect back on a situation that you received mercy from someone? Have you ever received a hundred dollar handshake? Have you ever had an appliance given to you that you needed? Have you been given an automobile? When you begin to reminisce about the act(s) of mercy that you have received, are you willing to pass the light of giving to others?

My husband was a pastor of a small rural church in Arizona one time, and on his day off he decided to repair the washing machine, in the parsonage, that had been leaking. He had it in pieces all over the kitchen floor when there was a knock on the back door. I went to the door and in walked one of the members of the church. She said, "Oh, my, why is my pastor fixing the washing machine?" He was still sitting on the floor saying that it needed fixing and that he knew how to repair appliances. She then said that she wanted to buy us a new washing machine and matching dryer. He gracefully declined, but thanked her for the offer. She seemed disappointed. Two weeks later the machine broke down again. He was embarrassed, so he asked me if I would call back to see if her offer was still good? She immediately said "Yes!" Two hours later a washing machine and dryer were delivered to the parsonage. Sometimes it is difficult to admit you need mercy given to you. Do not rob people of their blessings of giving to you.

This same lady called me several weeks later asking me to do her a favor. She wanted me to drive her to the commissary on an Air Force Base about 60 miles away. They needed to do their monthly shopping, and she did not want to drive that far alone. I agreed, and we started the drive together. She went into the commissary, and I had to wait outside. She took about an hour to shop, but she finally motioned me to bring my automobile to the front to load the groceries. She must have shopped for a month, because the car was loaded. We headed back, and I told her that I would drive her to her house. She said. "No, just to go on to your house." We pulled up, and she got out to go get my husband. He came out, and she then asked him to take the groceries into our home. I began to cry! This couple became our personal blessing, and we could never repay what they did for us privately. Their acts of giving and mercy were gems in their crowns that will someday be placed at the feet of Jesus. This couple took the command that Jesus said seriously when He said, "Go and do likewise". Mercy is receiving something you do not deserve and not getting what you do deserve.

The Whisper of Mercy

Let us come back to your story. You have just been reminded about what Jesus has described in the parable and you are sitting here talking to this couple a week later. They seem to be terribly remorseful for what they did to you. They admitted they were wrong, but they needed to eat. You asked them, "Why did you not tell us how desperate you were?" They said, "At first, we could not tell you, because we had just gotten to know you." They said, "You seemed to us that you had more than you needed, so we began to take things from your house. This really should not have given us a reason to steal, but it did." They continued to tell you that as soon as they found work, they would pay you back. You are softened by their story, but it is hard to trust this couple now. You decide not to call the police. You offered to help find them a job instead. You said that you would offer to buy them groceries until they found their jobs. You agreed to allow them to pay you back for the one thing that had not been returned, but that was all that you would accept.

You may decide differently in your own heart, but what is mercy? You may think that this couple needed to be punished. Yes, according to the law, they should be arrested and put in jail. Have you ever stolen something from someone? Have you been forgiven? Has this couple had more than their share of heartache? Would you be willing to share the love and truth about Jesus Christ?

Has Jesus forgiven you and stretched out His hand to offer you mercy? You may have robbed God of the fellowship He desires to have with you. You may not have trusted His heart to provide for you. Now is the time to accept His mercy and move forward with His strength in your heart. Listen for the whispers that ask you to offer a cup of water to someone, or a smile or needed groceries. Listen for the prompting asking you to give the last of your money until you get paid the next time. There is always an opportunity to show mercy, in the name of Jesus Christ, to someone that needs His love through you.

> *Matthew 25:31-40, "When the Son of Man comes in his glory, and all the angels with him, he will sit on his throne in heavenly glory. All the nations will be gathered before him, and he will separate the people one from another as a shepherd separates the sheep from the goats. He will put the sheep on his right and the goats on his left. "Then the King will say to those on his right, 'Come, you who are blessed by my Father; take your inheritance, the kingdom prepared for you since the creation of the world. For I was hungry and you gave me something to eat, I was thirsty and you gave me something to drink, I was a stranger and you invited me in, I needed clothes and you clothed me, I was sick and you looked after me, I was in prison and you came to visit me.' "Then the righteous will answer him, 'Lord, when did we see you hungry and feed you, or thirsty and give you something to drink? When did we see you a stranger and invite you in, or needing clothes and clothe you? When did we see you sick or in prison and go to visit you?' "The King will reply, 'I tell you the truth, whatever you did for one of the least of these brothers of mine, you did for me.' NIV*

Several times throughout the Bible people have cried out to God asking for His mercy. What were the circumstances the people faced? David cried out asking for mercy all through the book of Psalms. He had enemies who surrounded him many times during the wars he was fighting and prayed for God's mercy. (Psalms 6:9, Psalms 25:6 and Psalms 28:2-6) There are many more Scriptures, but these are a few that you can read for yourself. Daniel prayed for mercy so he and his friends would not be executed in Babylon. (Daniel 2:18) God answered their prayers in a mighty way and God's mercy was granted. God was glorified at the same time He showered down His mercy. Two blind men sitting on the roadside cried for Jesus to have mercy on them. (Matthew 20:30-31) Another man at the gate, who was blind, cried out for mercy (Matthew 10:47-48 & Luke 18:38-39). Jesus showed mercy and healed these blind men. Did they earn His mercy? No, but their faith in Jesus is what healed them.

Sometimes people did not deserve the mercy that God offered. Jesus poured down His mercy on to people, but He had the choice of whom He would bless. This is true today, and there is another parable that explains the reason for His choices. (Luke 18:9-14) The tax collector pounded on his chest asking God to have mercy on him, a sinner. Jesus sat on a mountainside and taught His greatest message. We call it the Sermon on the Mount. One of the Beatitudes is found in Matthew 5:7, *"Blessed are the merciful, for they will be shown mercy." NIV*

Jesus Christ not only gave you grace when He died on the cross of Calvary, but he demonstrated the ultimate gift of mercy that was ever offered. His cry from the cross, *"It is finished"* was for grace and His words found in (Luke 23:34) *Jesus said, "Father, forgive them, for they do not know what they are doing." NIV.* These were the words that gave you His mercy.

1. *Pray:*

Lord, I know that I have not deserved your mercy due to the sins I have committed in the past and on a daily basis, so I am asking for forgiveness and continued mercy. Please show me to reflect your mercy on everyone that I meet. I know that sometimes I will fail to recognize the need to express your mercy, so please prompt me by the power of the Holy Spirit to alert my heart to do what is right. Thank you for not giving me what I truly deserve, which is your wrath.

2. *Reflection:*

What have you learned about mercy? Are you willing to express God's mercy when people do not deserve it?

CHAPTER 12

The Whisper of a Divine Secret

Psalms 119:105, "Your word is a lamp to my feet and a light for my path." NIV

We are going to take another fictional journey together and walk a path to the greatest secret that could be given to humanity. Your life is full of disappointments, but you keep trying. You want to give up, but what would that do for you or for your family? You feel you are walking alone in a dark alley late at night. You ask yourself, "What is ahead?" You are trying to clear your head at what to do next in this journey through life. Memories are coming back into your head as you continue to walk down this alley. The alley opens up to the long dark road ahead, but you just keep walking. Your first memory is of your childhood. What was exciting about growing up? You dismiss those thoughts and turn to your disappointments. Your dad beat your mother! Why could you not stop him? Your dad left you and your mother. He never came back home. Where did he go? Oh, you hate your dad! You cannot change what happened, but it still haunts you because your mother worked so hard to make a home for you. Your mother married again, and the new dad in your life was nice at first. Then he began to beat you. He told you not to tell your mother, but then he finally left, too. You ask yourself, "Is there something wrong with me?" You keep thinking that school was a favorite get-a-way due to the friends you had. Where were they now? They moved on with their lives just like you did. You worked hard to get a college education. It took you eight years instead of four years because you worked three jobs to make ends meet. You met your spouse and a bright new future began. You were married, you finally had a good job and then your first child was born. You and your family were excited about your future. Your boss was on you all the time for not following the rules of the company. You attempted to tell him that there were new ideas out there that are working and that you wanted to try to better the company. He said, "It is his way or the highway for you!" You are put on probation for thirty days. You better not think about new ideas but just do what you are told. The thirty days passed, and it was not enough to convince the boss that you were worth keeping as an employee. What now?

You are walking down a dark road physically and mentally. There is a light ahead, but it seems a long way off. The negative thoughts keep surfacing in your memories. You are trying not to remember things that have disappointed you, but it is a struggle. You keep walking the road towards this light, but what is drawing you? You remember one time, when you were twelve years old, that someone invited you to church. You remember a warm fuzzy feeling when you bowed your head to pray asking Jesus to come into your heart. You ask, "How did that memory pop into your head?" You had never attended church again.

You stumble over something in the road, and it is a bright pebble. You pick up the pebble, and then something whispers to you, "Let go of the negative memory of what your Father said and did to you!" You turned around to see if there was someone close to you. Nothing! It was still dark! Forgive my father? How could I; he left. The whisper came again, "Let the memories of your Father's abuse go because it is in the past!" You drop to your knees and weep. You realize this is controlling your thoughts, and you have to let it go. You had nothing to do with him leaving. You stand up and walk on further. A slight burden has lifted, and you start to feel fresh. You drop the pebble and leave it on the road.

There is another stone on the ground and it is a little bigger. You look up and the light ahead is still quite a distance. The whisper came again,

"Forgive your mother." Why? What has she done wrong? The whisper said again, "Your mother married someone who attempted be a father to you, and consistently punished you. Please attempt to understand that this man loved your mom." " Release the memory of what your mother did, because it is in the past!" You did not have control over what happened to you or control over what people did to you. Are you going to live in the past or live to a brighter future? You may think that there could never be a brighter future for you. You take a chance and desire to forgive your mother. You seem to be lighter on your feet.

You keep walking and another whisper comes into your heart. "You should be thankful you decided to get an education in spite of your odds for not trying." You had always been asking yourself if it was worth getting the education because it was such a struggle. "You need to see the bigger picture and forgive yourself!" You finally realize that you were too hard on yourself. You need to forgive your past and another person. YOU! You fall to the ground in tears after having decided to forgive yourself!

When you get up, you notice the light in the distance is getting closer, so you keep walking. You noticed that your steps were almost like skipping. Wow! You are beginning to like how you were feeling.

There is another bright pebble, so you pick it up. The whisper came again, "Forgive your boss for firing you!" Now that is a hard one because he never gave you a chance to prove that you could be beneficial to his company. "The whisper said, that was in the past and besides he was jealous of your ideas!" You decided that maybe some people do not like change, so you need to accept people for who they are. You ask, "Where did thought come from and who put that thought in your head?" You decide to forgive your boss, so you tell yourself that there may be a better job out there that can use your talent and training.

The burdens are lighter than you ever expected to experience. With every pebble, rock or stone you picked up you throw it away right after you decide to forgive what had happened in the past. You decide that you cannot change the past, but how do you go forward into the future? You realize that the whispers were from God.

Matthew 6:14-15, "For if you forgive men when they sin against you, your heavenly Father will also forgive you. But if you do not forgive men their sins, your Father will not forgive your sins." NIV

God Forgives You

Romans 10:9-13, "… if you confess with your mouth, 'Jesus is Lord,' and believe in your heart that God raised him from the dead, you will be saved. For it is with your heart that you believe and are justified, and it is with your mouth that you confess and are saved. As the Scripture says, 'Anyone who trusts in him will never be put to shame.' For there is no difference between Jew and Gentile — the same Lord is Lord of all and richly blesses all who call on him, for, 'Everyone who calls on the name of the Lord will be saved.'" NIV

You start to focus on that day in church when someone told you how you could be saved. You remember that you talked to God about your sins asking Him to forgive you. Did He really forgive you? Did you truly mean that you wanted to be forgiven? What had your attitude been when you were twelve? Did you blame everybody around you for all the things that were happening to you, or did you blame yourself? You began to remember you wanted to be forgiven for your attitude. God did forgive you! You had not realized, until this walk, that you had not forgiven others who had mistreated you. When you made the choice to forgive those people, you were at peace, so what is the next step? You hear another whisper, and it said. "Learn about me." Does that mean that you must learn about the message that God wants you to understand?

You continued to walk and began remembering a friend that had worked with you and they had invited you to their church. This could be a new beginning if you call this person when you get back home. You turn around to realize that you were a long way from home. You look towards the light and kept walking. Maybe that light is a house. You could use the telephone to call your spouse to come and get you.

You see another bright stone, and you hear the whisper, "I forgive you! Go and sin no more!" You drop the stone and drop to your knees, weeping, asking God to forgive you for yours sins and to give you His wisdom that will help you to sin no more! You pray and tell God that you are weak and you need His strength to do what is right in His eyes. Your heart is at peace knowing that God heard your prayers. You get up and keep walking.

Your memory of your spouse and your child came to your mind. You ask yourself if they were worried about being gone so long. You pick up your pace and trip over a bolder in the road. You fall flat on your face! You said, "I did not see that bolder in the road!" It had not been bright enough for you to be able to see. While you lay there, another whisper came to you, "The enemy will attempt to trip you and make you fall." This frightens you, but you thank the Lord for His warning. You get up, dust yourself off and walk towards the light again.

> *1 Peter 5:8-11, Be sober, be vigilant; because your adversary the devil walks about like a roaring lion, seeking whom he may devour. Resist him, steadfast in the faith, knowing that the same sufferings are experienced by your brotherhood in the world. But may the God of all grace, who called us to His eternal glory by Christ Jesus, after you have suffered a while, perfect, establish, strengthen, and settle you. To Him be the glory and the dominion forever and ever. Amen. NKJV*

You began to skip along the road remembering that God has forgiven you!

How Many Times Must You Forgive?

> *Matthew 18:21-22, Then Peter came to Jesus and asked, "Lord, how many times shall I forgive my brother when he sins against me? Up to seven times?" Jesus answered, "I tell you, not seven times, but seventy-seven times. NIV*

You are getting weary from all this walking. The path is long and dark, but you have not tripped and have not seen any more rocks that shine in the dark. The light ahead is still there, but it does not seem to be getting any brighter. You begin the think about your friends and enemies in high school and college who stressed you out. This one professor failed you, and you had to take the class again. You had to see his face everyday in class knowing that he failed you the previous semester. He seemed to always talk down to you. Some of your acquaintances were not encouraging and called you a nerd. You remember your stepfather telling you that you would never amount to anything. You have memories of your mother yelling at you for not doing your homework or your chores. Your friend was always wanting that special guy or girl for themselves that you were dating. You realize that he or she was really not a friend, but a user. You began to get angry for all those people that continue to trip you, hurt you or call you names. Oh, yes, what about that position that you wanted and another friend got the job? Just as fast as those memories filled your mind, you tripped again, but this time there are rocks all over the place. The road has turned rocky! You reach out to grab something to pull you up and you fall again.

You just lie in that pile of rock and it is very quiet and dark. The whisper came again and said, "You will have to forgive the same people for many reasons, over and over again." You think, "This is just not fair. Why do I have to forgive these nasty people?" The answer came back, "These memories keep you in bondage, and you are in slavery. True forgiveness is when you let go of the offense and choose to forget." You say to yourself, "That is shocking information. I did not realize that!" You realize that your anger really did not hurt them but was actually hurting you. When you forget the offense, you release the memory of the pain. Releasing the negative memories will make room for more positive experiences. You pray again, "Lord help me to forgive those that have hurt me in the past and may even hurt me in the future." You remember that Jesus said to forgive seventy-seven times, but you are only human. You asked God to help you in your weakness. You began the new journey, in your heart, to forgive more people. The choice to forgive helps you to grow up emotionally and spiritually. Do you want to remain a child? Yes, you must come to Jesus like a child, but He will help you mature.

You decide to give your weakness to the Lord and slowly get up off the ground. The path became smooth again, but you began to be careful to where you were walking. This world is dark, but the light of Jesus Christ is the light that will make your path bright. He will give you understanding and wisdom as you take each new step in the direction to forgive others.

> *Matthew 10:27-30, "What I tell you in the dark, speak in*
> *the daylight; what is whispered in your ear, proclaim from the*
> *roofs. Do not be afraid of those who kill the body but cannot*
> *kill the soul. Rather, be afraid of the One who can destroy*
> *both soul and body in hell. Are not two sparrows sold for a*
> *penny? Yet not one of them will fall to the ground apart from*
> *the will of your Father. And even the very hairs of your head*
> *are all numbered. So don't be afraid; you are worth more*
> *than many sparrows." NIV*

God Can Help!

> *Psalms 121:2, "My help comes from the Lord, the Maker of*
> *heaven and earth." NIV*

Your mind has been given a new revelation from God, but soon you will be back looking for a new job. You will face future days of challenges and uncertainty, but you are at peace. How can you possibly share what has happened to you during this walk? Will your spouse believe where you have been? How do you begin to speak of the wonders of these whispers? You are humbled that you have been shown how special you are to God. You want others to know how special they are to God. You begin to think that some people will make fun of you, or even be critical. There are some people who will not believe what you experienced because they have known you all your life. Do you keep this journey a secret because people will reject what you are saying? How are you to make this decision? You see another bright stone in the road and this time you run to pick it up! The whisper said, "You are never going to be alone, and I will be with you." Your thoughts generate another message saying, "Jesus will whisper to my heart what needs to be said to others." Your walk through the dark path of learning to forgive has been difficult, but the Lord has guided you with the light of wisdom that leads to spiritual freedom.

You remember that you were told that when you do not forgive, you are in bondage. The memory of the wrong done to you controls you and your thinking. You are in the jail of memories that have happened in the past that you have no control over. You need to let go and let God give you His future that He has planned for you.

You realize that your thinking has to change and that it will take time to make the adjustments to give you the hope that you desire. You know that it took you a long time to get your college education and that you did not learn your trade overnight without studying. You had to read and learn what would give you the profession of your choice. You have been given a new direction, and this will require studying the Bible to learn about the character and will of God. You need to give God the time that will help you grow in your new faith. You know you must join a church and a Bible Study Class to help you learn. Will you listen to give a response to when someone is teaching, in the future, or to gain understanding? This will be your choice.

The light is getting brighter and closer to you now. The road is still dark, but you know that God will help you.

> *Matthew 7:13-14, "Enter through the narrow gate. For wide is the gate and broad is the road that leads to destruction, and many enter through it. But small is the gate and narrow the road that leads to life, and only a few find it." NIV*

Jesus Shares the Secret

> *John 13:34-35, "A new command I give you: Love one another. As I have loved you, so you must love one another. By this all men will know that you are my disciples, if you love one another." NIV*

The light is getting closer now, and it is a very short walk to the door where this light has guided you. You trip again on the road before you get to the door, but this time you catch yourself from falling to the ground. What was that you tripped over? You see a brick that was broken off from the steps going into the building. The brick is too heavy for you to pick up and throw it out of the way. You notice, in the light of the building, that there is a footprint embedded in the brick. Someone must have been here when the building was built and stepped into wet cement. It definitely is a footprint. You are thinking that maybe there have been other people, like you, who have walked the pathway to this building. You wonder who the first person was and what was the purpose? You kneel down to look closer to the footprint and another whisper says to you, "I walked a dark road once for you, and I am in the building waiting for you to come to me." Who is this person? You walked up the steps and opened the door. There is the brightest light you have ever seen. Standing there in the middle of the room was 'Jesus'. He said, "Come to me and I will share more about the secret of forgiveness that will set you free." You learn that while you were taking this walk down this dark road your family was taking a similar walk of their own. You listen to understand that it is Jesus that invites people to see the light of His truth. He is the light and the truth that brightens our world. He told you that you must love your brothers and sisters.

Jesus asks you to sit at His feet as He shares with you the message of acceptance. He tells you that there will be others arriving soon. He wants you to take His yoke upon you and learn of Him. He said that His burden would be very light to carry. He does not want you to carry your burdens anymore because they have caused you to drag your feet. There are heavy stones that you have been carrying in your life. He wants you throw to those pebbles, stones, heavy bricks at His feet. He begins to tell you that He died for you and took your sins on His shoulders so that you could be forgiven. You remember that you have already asked God to forgive your sins and now you understand why.

You ask Jesus if there is a phone in the building to be able to call your family. You need a ride home. Jesus said, "You do not need a telephone".

You are suddenly awakened out of your deep sleep. You say to yourself, "Was the walk down that dark road real? You will never forget the dream. You get up scrambling to find your Bible to look up the Scriptures that were revealed to you in this dream. The messages of the Scriptures are real! Your spouse asks you what was going on and you tell your spouse that it is a long story. You tell him or her that you had a dream that has changed your life forever.

This has been a fictional story, but the truth is that we all live in a dark world. We sometimes have to walk down a dark path to the see light of God's whispers at times. My path was the path of cancer and recovery. Do you think that maybe I might have learned more about God's love because of the path that He asked me to walk? The path is to forgive those who have mistreated you. Some people have acted out of their own ignorance. People sometimes do not realize that they have hurt you, so you need to make a choice to forget the negative memories. Jesus said to love one another but not just those that love us. It is easy for us to love those who love us, but it is difficult to love those who are not so lovely. We need to ask Jesus to give us the Holy Spirit's power to learn to love those who do not love us. This is not humanly possible due to our sinful nature.

You need to take a mental flight to the top of the cross to see what Jesus was seeing as He hung on that tree. The crowd was looking at Him and His mother standing at His feet with His favorite disciple. You see some people crying and holding each other. You see the Roman soldiers casting lots for His robe, and then you see one of them pierce His side with a spear. He never cries out for himself, but He asks God the Father to forgive everyone. When you watch what happened, can you learn to forgive others as Jesus forgave you? Will you make a choice to sit at the feet of Jesus to listen for understanding of the truth that He desires to share with you?

You can sit at the feet of Jesus and listen to His teaching today by opening up your Bible daily to read His words. Do you really want to read so that you have something to talk about or learn the deeper meaning of His truth? Listen for the whispers to understand the secrets that Jesus wants to share with you.

John 8:31-32, To the Jews who had believed him, Jesus said,
"If you hold to my teaching, you are really my disciples. Then
you will know the truth, and the truth will set you free." NIV

1. *Pray:*

Lord, forgive me for I have sinned. I have sinned against YOU and brothers and sisters that have disappointed me. Your Word says that if we do not forgive people, the Heavenly Father will not forgive us. Teach me to forgive offenses immediately, because my human heart wants to carry grudges. Change me, Lord, to forgive as you have forgiven me.

2. *Reflection:*

Do you have someone to forgive? Do you have an experience to forget by the spiritual gift ability to forgive? Do you believe that God will teach you how to forgive by Jesus Christ example?

CHAPTER 13

The Whisper Through the Seasons of Life

Have you ever sat alone in a room and just began to remember your experiences as a child, a teenager, a young adult, a median adult? You may be in the season of being a senior adult? What were your thoughts about God and how did you respond to circumstances that have happened during these seasons of life? Do you remember the people that you called friends and are they still in your life? Today there is Facebook and some friends may have reconnected with you. Have some of your friends changed? Have you changed mentally, physically or spiritually? You have shared life experiences with many of these friends, but life moves on to other challenges. You may have moved away from where you grew up or your friends may have moved on.

Do you remember a time as a child when you should have been killed and something wonderful happened that changed the outcome of a possible tragedy? What happened and what changed the situation? When you were a teenager, did somebody care about how you felt, or did someone guide you on to a path that changed your life's dream? Could a teacher, a friend's mother or father, care about you? Maybe there was someone else that you thought would never make an impact on your life?

What about when you were a young adult? Did an employer give you a chance to prove yourself in a job you really wanted? What about a possible chance to go to college, when you thought the possibility was very slim. Little by little, your life began to change for the better, but not without disappointments. Right? The moment you realized that there truly was a God that loved you, your life may have taken on a different path then what you wanted for yourself. The message of this chapter tells all believers that there is a plan for your life, but it may take some of the seasons of your life to witness the power of a caring God. He will not give all that you need to know about Him in one single season of your life, but it is His whisper's to your heart, that will make you go a different direction at different times. His timing is perfect and His wisdom will be understood as your grow spiritually. He will reveal Himself to you one day at a time, through the up's and down's, of your life.

> *Ecclesiastes 3:1-8, There is a time for everything, and a season for every activity under heaven: a time to be born and a time to die, a time to plant and a time to uproot, a time to kill and a time to heal, a time to tear down and a time to build, a time to weep and a time to laugh, a time to mourn and a time to dance, a time to scatter stones and a time to gather them, a time to embrace and a time to refrain, a time to search and a time to give up, a time to keep and a time to throw away, a time to tear and a time to mend, a time to be silent and a time to speak, a time to love and a time to hate, a time for war and a time for peace. NIV*

Just to stir your thinking for a moment with a question. Where were you or what were you doing when the Twin Towers in Manhattan, New York were destroyed? What were you doing when you or where were you when you said "yes" to Jesus Christ, accepting Him as your Lord and Savior? Do you remember both experiences? Both these powerful experiences have changed your thinking and your life. These experiences are different for everyone that remembers. Jesus Christ has touched humanity in a personal and real way to each man, woman or child, that is unique to them. Let us journey together with the people in the Bible God introduced Himself to an individual for a unique reason.

Who was queen Esther?

Queen Esther was a hero to her people when women were considered less than human in the eyes of her nation. Esther was a young beautiful Jewish girl who just happened have been chosen as the new queen for king Xerxes. Her true identity was not revealed to the king at the time she was chosen. She was in the right place at the right time in history to assist in saving her people from destruction. She was told by her uncle Mordecai to keep her family background a secret.

Mordecai had over heard two of the king's officers talking about killing king Xerxes.

> *Esther 2:19-23, When the virgins were assembled a second time, Mordecai was sitting at the king's gate. But Esther had kept secret her family background and nationality just as Mordecai had told her to do, for she continued to follow Mordecai's instructions as she had done when he was bringing her up. During the time Mordecai was sitting at the king's gate, Bigthana and Teresh, two of the king's officers who guarded the doorway, became angry and conspired to assassinate King Xerxes. But Mordecai found out about the plot and told Queen Esther, who in turn reported it to the king, giving credit to Mordecai. And when the report was investigated and found to be true, the two officials were hanged on a gallows. All this was recorded in the book of the annals in the presence of the king. NIV*

Did you notice that queen Esther honored her uncle's instructions, as she had always done as child growing up in his home, and to save the king she had just married? Esther's father had died when she was a young girl, so Mordecai raised her as his own daughter. Esther did not choose the family that would raise her nor did she choose neither her family background nor her nationality. Did she? Who made that choice? The Holy God of

Israel made the choice for her and placed her in the exact position that would protect the future of His chosen people. The entire story of Esther was in a time where the Jewish people were being killed and there were underlining leaders conspiring to wipeout this group of believers. The Jewish people's success has attracted so much jealousy that a powerful man named Haman, conspired to trick king Xerxes into signing a document to destroy the people who he was saying was not obeying the king's laws. The message was sent by couriers to all the king's provinces with orders to kill and annihilate all the Jews – young and old, women and young children on a certain day. They were to plunder all their goods. Mordecai heard about this decree and went to Queen Esther privately. He prayed, tore his clothes, put on sack clothes and ashes and cried in wails of torment to his Holy God. Queen Esther took action by revealing the plot to the king and than revealed her nationality to him. She approached the king knowing that she might be killed, but the king accepted her approach to him and heard her plea for her people. Later, Haman would be hanged and Mordecai would be honored. The people were not destroyed because of a faithful servant of God. Mordecai and Esther trusted in a Holy God that had a plan for their lives.

Esther grew up knowing that she was a humble Jewish girl, raised to understand her faith, but not knowing what the future would hold for her and her people. God had prepared her heart and her life for a time in history that would change the direction of His people.

You may be thinking, "Now how does this apply to my life in today's world?" First, does God have the right to place you where He wants you to be today? Could you be chosen to stand firm in your faith when the time is right to do what is right for the benefit of the people that are close to you?

What if you were hired to be a manager of a local business and there was another person in the business that wanted the job. This person had worked for the company for ten years and knew that they could do the job better than any new person that could be hired. You were told by the Administration that the reason you were hired is because of the your past experience of being honest, trustworthy and your desire to live a life of faith. This person, who wanted the job, began stealing from the company. Eventually this person went to the Administration stating his concerns regarding missing money or equipment. They said that it began happening around the time that you were hired. The Administration called you in to question these acquisitions. You told the Administration that you would follow-up and check what may have been stolen. Another employee came to you and told you about somebody stealing from the company. This other employee would now become a witness of what was going on and went to the Administration of what they had seen. Your accuser was fired. Your integrity was rewarded and trust was regained. You chose not to retaliate nor did you accuse the other employee. You trusted that God would reveal the truth and the company would be protected. You had been groomed to become a manager of integrity. People will listen when you become a person that lives their faith to honor God. Wait for God's timing, wisdom and His strength. Keep the light shining that is within you as a believer. That is what queen Esther did and she was a simple Jewish girl.

> *Matthew 5:14-16, "You are the light of the world. A city on a hill cannot be hidden. Neither do people light a lamp and put it under a bowl. Instead they put it on its stand, and it gives light to everyone in the house. In the same way, let your light shine before men, that they may see your good deeds and praise your Father in heaven. NIV*

Who was Moses?

There was a time in history that the land of Egypt was ruled by what was called a Pharaoh. God's people had migrated to Egypt during a fathom in their land many years prior and had grown in number. There was a new Pharaoh that came to rule and became concerned with the numbers of the foreign people that lived in his land. He was ruthless and demanded hardship to these people. He even instructed the midwives to destroy all baby boys to be killed at birth to keep the people from getting stronger. The Israelite midwives feared God and refused to destroy the newborn baby boys. This angered the new Pharaoh, so he demanded that the young boys be thrown in the Nile River. (Exodus 1:1-16)

Then a man and his wife from the Levites had a son. The wife saw that this child was special, so she hid him for three months. Out of her desire to save her son she made a small water safe basket to put him in and gently placed him in the basket. She turned to her daughter to watch him as he was placed in the flowing water of the Nile passing by where the Pharaoh's daughter was standing. The older sister watched from a distance and ran to the Pharaoh's daughter to tell her that she knew a Hebrew woman That could nurse him until he was weaned. She agreed and the Israelite woman nursed him until he was weaned and then retuned him the Pharaoh's daughter. The Pharaoh's daughter named him "Moses".

When Moses grew to be a young adult, living in the home of the Pharaoh, He was witnessing the cruelty of his people by the Egyptians. One day he saw two Egyptians severely beating a Israelite slave, so looking around, he saw no one watching, he killed the two Egyptians. The next day he saw two Israelites fighting and told them to stop fighting. The asked him, "Who made you our ruler when you killed two Egyptians?" He knew that this news would reach the Pharaoh, so he fled this land and ended up in a place called Midian. (Exodus 2:1-10)

Moses met his new family in Midian and became a shepherd over the next 40 years. He married and had a family of his own. He watched and cared for many flocks of sheep, learning to become the leader that he would one day become for God. He was being prepared in way that would one day honor and deliver His people from slavery. God had prepared Moses through many seasons of his life where he would hear the whisper of God.

Moses was tending the sheep of his father-in-law Jethro when he saw burning bush that was not being consumed by the blaze. He walked closer when he heard a voice coming from the burning bush.

Exodus 3:7-15, And the Lord said: "I have surely seen the oppression of My people who are in Egypt, and have heard their cry because of their taskmasters, for I know their sorrows. So I have come down to deliver them out of the hand of the Egyptians, and to bring them up from that land to a good and large land, to a land flowing with milk and honey, to the place of the Canaanites and the Hittites and the Amorites and the Perizzites and the Hivites and the Jebusites. Now therefore, behold, the cry of the children of Israel has come to Me, and I have also seen the oppression with which the

Egyptians oppress them. Come now, therefore, and I will send you to Pharaoh that you may bring My people, the children of Israel, out of Egypt." But Moses said to God, "Who am I that I should go to Pharaoh, and that I should bring the children of Israel out of Egypt?" So He said, "I will certainly be with you. And this shall be a sign to you that I have sent you: When you have brought the people out of Egypt, you shall serve God on this mountain." Then Moses said to God, "Indeed, when I come to the children of Israel and say to them, 'The God of your fathers has sent me to you,' and they say to me, 'What is His name?' what shall I say to them?" And God said to Moses, "I AM WHO I AM." And He said, "Thus you shall say to the children of Israel, 'I AM has sent me to you.'" NKJV

Moses had been saved as a baby, brought into the Pharaoh home to be raised, and then fled to Midian to live for the next 40 years. God knew Moses was prepared to help set God's people free the bondage of slavery. Moses did as the Lord commanded him to do and much more in obedience to God's plan and will for the people of God.

How does this apply to us today? Are you an Israelite, or are you a slave, or are you having difficult time that you are facing today? Could you be in bondage to someone or have you placed some bondage on yourself? Have you ever said, "My life is of no earthly value?" Who gave you the right to say something like that, or even think it? Think about the seasons of your life and what EXPERIENCES have you had that could prepare you for a whisper from a Holy God? It took Moses 40 years to hear a life-changing message from God. Wasn't Moses just human, like you are? What made him different? Wasn't it the plan and power of the Creator working through Moses that made him different? Moses could of never accomplished the activity he followed through without the majestic power of God!

Did Moses choose where he born, who he born to or what he ended up doing for God. The only choice that Moses made was eventually to be obedient to the command of the Lord. The Lord God carried Moses to a high mountain where he allowed God to carve the commandments of God in stone. The people would now have a message from God that would bring

His people into a relationship with Him. The people would not always be faithful, but what about those that would be faithful in the future?

Would you be one of those that would be faithful and listen for the whisper of God to go forth and be obedient to God's command? When you accepted Jesus as your Lord and Savior, you were given the Holy Spirit. You have been given the gift of communication and his voice is simply a whisper. He has been speaking to you through the circumstances of your life, or the seasons of your life, and now you may be ready to listen. His words are life and or not meant to destroy you. Jesus speaks of the destroyer and not to listen to this voice.

> *John 10:1-10, "I tell you the truth, the man who does not enter the sheep pen by the gate, but climbs in by some other way, is a thief and a robber. The man who enters by the gate is the shepherd of his sheep. The watchman opens the gate for him, and the sheep listen to his voice. He calls his own sheep by name and leads them out. When he has brought out all his own, he goes on ahead of them, and his sheep follow him because they **know his voice**. But they will never follow a stranger; in fact, they will run away from him because **they do not recognize a stranger's voice**." Jesus used this figure of speech, but they did not understand what he was telling them. Therefore Jesus said again, "I tell you the truth, I am the gate for the sheep. All who ever came before me were thieves and robbers, but the sheep did not listen to them. I am the gate; whoever enters through me will be saved. He will come in and go out, and find pasture. The thief comes only to steal and kill and destroy; I have come that they may have life, and have it to the fullest. NIV*

He may ask you to walk before the chosen people to lead them to life abundantly, but maybe not like He did Moses. This was the activity of God once in history and we have learned that God has a plan for His people. One by one, and one moment at a time, He will whisper His love to you as you become faithful in trusting in God's passionate heart.

Who was Paul?

Paul was an amazing man of faith who wrote most of the books in the New Testament after the Gospels were written. He wrote letters to encourage the new organized churches as he traveled. The Bible tells of all of his missionary journeys through years of suffering to share the truth of Jesus Christ. His life is an encouragement for all of us who believe today. The missionary journeys took many years to accomplish, but he maintained his faith. Paul, who once was Saul, from the Tribe of Benjamin, he had been circumcised on the eighth day, as was a custom of the Jewish faith. He was a Hebrews of Hebrews: in regards to the law and a Pharisee. (Philippians 3:4-6)

You may ask why include "Who was Paul" in this chapter? His story is worth repeating in this book, because of the power of Paul's testimony. Paul has inspired us all to keep pressing forward in our faith in Jesus Christ, carrying a thorn in his flesh. There was an aliment that most scholars debate about as to what it was he suffered from? The Bible tells us that Paul encountered the powerful presence of the resurrected Jesus Christ on the road to Damascus, who struck him blind. He was on his way to persecute the new believers in Jesus Christ. (Acts 9:1-19) The whisper, that only he heard, changed Paul's life forever. Once he understood the message he quickly became obedient to the actions he would now follow.

Acts 9:3-9, As he neared Damascus on his journey, suddenly a light from heaven flashed around him. He fell to the ground and heard a voice say to him, **"Saul, Saul, why do you persecute me?"** *"Who are you, Lord?" Saul asked.* **"I am Jesus, whom you are persecuting,"** *he replied.* **"Now get up and go into the city, and you will be told what you must do."** *The men traveling with Saul stood there speechless; they heard the sound but did not see anyone. Saul got up from the ground, but when he opened his eyes he could see nothing. So they led him by the hand into Damascus. For three days he was blind, and did not eat or drink anything. NIV*

When Saul heard the voice of the Lord, he became obedient, and assisted in changing our world as believers. He suffered of all kinds of physical trials to spread the truth of Jesus Christ, who He was and what He did for us on the cross of Calvary.

Our family lived in Italy for a period of time and we took a journey to Rome. We toured St. Peter's Basilica, the Sistine Chapel and many other churches in the area, but there were two places that left a lasting impression on our lives. Today, tourist cannot go underground to view the Catacombs where many of the first believers are buried. As we walked through these Catacombs the presence of the Lord was felt in our hearts. Neither of us were saved at the time, but within six months after this experience, we came to know the Lord personally. The second experience was one of Paul 's prison cells where he wrote one of the letters that we have in our Bible today. The cell was underground and a small straight up and down ladder was the only entrance. The cell was all rock enclosed with hand and ankle chains embedded in the rounded prison. The prison was about 15 feet in diameter. In the left hand side of the prison was a rock shelf where a candle was placed to bring some light to this dark dungeon. This was where Paul was allowed to write the letter(s). This experience was a season in our family's lives that would make a permanent impression in our hearts. The Bible became real for us that day and the words that Paul would write would change our hearts forever. Paul writes these Scriptures in the letter to the Philippians.

> *Philippians 4:4-13, Rejoice in the Lord always. Again I will say, rejoice! Let your gentleness be known to all men. The Lord is at hand. Be anxious for nothing, but in everything by prayer and supplication, with thanksgiving, let your requests be made known to God; and the peace of God, which surpasses all understanding, will guard your hearts and minds through Christ Jesus.*

Meditate on These Things

> *Finally, brethren, whatever things are true, whatever things are noble, whatever things are just, whatever things are pure, whatever things are lovely, whatever things are of good report, if there is any virtue and if there is anything praiseworthy*

— meditate on these things. The things which you learned and received and heard and saw in me, these do, and the God of peace will be with you. But I rejoiced in the Lord greatly that now at last your care for me has flourished again; though you surely did care, but you lacked opportunity. Not that I speak in regard to need, for I have learned in whatever state I am, to be content: I know how to be abased, and I know how to abound. Everywhere and in all things I have learned both to be full and to be hungry, both to abound and to suffer need. I can do all things through Christ who strengthens me. NKJV.

What an amazing message Paul gave to humanity while he was imprisoned in Rome, Italy!

The Simple Whisper through Circumstances

You have just been introduced to two Biblical characters and how God worked through their lives to protect His people. The stories are not about the people as much as it is about the character of God. He is passionate, but He does not tolerate a disobedient believer. He will discipline those He loves, because they are on a personal destructive path that will cause grief. First, the path of unforgiveness that destroys relationships and the individual(s) that will not forgive. Some people live in a bittersweet world, at times, and turn against someone that they really loved at one time. Harsh words can be said and misunderstood. Stop and try to remember that Jesus cried from the cross and said, "Forgive them, Father, for they know not what they do!" You are not divine your natural state, because you are human and sinful in nature. Jesus will whisper to your heart on how to forgive as He has forgiven you, when you humble your heart to listening for His words. You are probably wondering why I bring this kind of circumstance up in the writing regarding the seasons of life? Just recently three people have revealed to me their unwillingness to forgive another believer. The pain was real and the anger for those people have hardened their hearts. We all experience this in our life. This will stifle the power of the Lord working through your life. What does the Word tell us should be like and how we allow the character of God to reveal His ways?

> *Colossians 3:12-17, Therefore, as the elect of God, holy and beloved, put on tender mercies, kindness, humility, meekness, longsuffering; bearing with one another, and forgiving one another, if anyone has a complaint against another; even as Christ forgave you, so you also must do. But above all these things put on love, which is the bond of perfection. And let the peace of God rule in your hearts, to which also you were called in one body; and be thankful. Let the word of Christ dwell in you richly in all wisdom, teaching and admonishing one another in psalms and hymns and spiritual songs, singing with grace in your hearts to the Lord. And whatever you do in word or deed, do all in the name of the Lord Jesus, giving thanks to God the Father through Him. NKJV*

As believers you have experienced the touch of God that has directed your path through the seasons of life. When you have fallen, it may not have been as bad as it could have been. When you do not get your way, thank Him, and when you are disappointed, thank Him. When you receive blessings more than you could ever imagine, Thank and Praise Him. The circumstance through the seasons of your life does not have to control you into having a bitter memory. Take a long look at your past with a heart that recognizes the touch of God's Holy Spirit. Did he keep you from having accident somewhere along the journey? Did you break up with a boy friend or a girl friend that could not have been a path of peace for if you had stayed with them? Thank God for those unanswered prayers. Have you wanted a job and then find out later the company had gone bankrupt? Have you been disappointed because you did get a house you wanted and than a week later you were offered a job in another city?

What about the times you may felt like God was not there for you in your circumstances? This was a time when the enemy has opportunity to lie to you. Remember that Jesus said that He is liar and a destroyer. Do you have someone in your life that you know that would always love you no matter what you say or do? You may have a father, a mother, a grandmother, a grandfather, or a friend? They are just human and they are not as passionate as the Holy God. Remember He loves and has your best interest in mind, even if you cannot physically see it through your circumstances. It is blind faith, but this faith will carry you through the disappointments. You will come out on the other end with stronger faith and knowing the character of God just a little bit better. Esther and Moses did not know the outcome of their circumstances, but they trusted God to be with them. You read the encounters and see how God was working. That is easy and it easy to see how has worked in your lives in the past, but what about today? Has God's Holy Spirit changed His passion for you? Remember that God placed you in the family you have, He chose the parents that you have and He will guide your path. His words can be simply a whisper to your heart from His heart.

> *1 Peter 4:7-11, The end of all things is near. Therefore be clear minded and self-controlled so that you can pray. Above all, love each other deeply, because love covers over a multitude of sins. Offer hospitality to one another without grumbling. Each one should use whatever gift he has received to serve others, faithfully administering God's grace in its various forms. If anyone speaks, he should do it as one speaking the very words of God. If anyone serves, he should do it with the strength God provides, so that in all things God may be praised through Jesus Christ. To him be the glory and the power for ever and ever. Amen. NIV*

1. *Pray:*
   Lord, I know that there have been seasons of my life that I am not proud in regard to my actions and attitude. I know that you have forgiven me. Help to see how you have guided and planned the activity to get to know you better. The ups and downs were planned, but not to harm me, but teach me to trust you more every day of my life.

2. *Reflection:*
   Do you remember how God has touched you through the seasons of your life? Keep a journal and you will begin to recognize His whispers every day.

CHAPTER 14

The Whisper of God from My Heart to Your Heart

I would like to introduce to you some of the devotionals that the Holy Spirit encouraged me to write. These are some of the whispers that have come from the Holy Spirit of God to my heart. I am calling them "FRESH START TODAY", because each new day can be a new beginning in your relationship with God. These devotionals are meant to encourage you to begin to write down your own whispers with God. If you have been blessed by reading this book, then I am inviting you to continue reading these devotionals by going to http://lenni-nord.blogspot.com. The devotionals are not written everyday, but they may be in the future as the Holy Spirit prompts me to write. Here are just a few that I have written, and I pray that God will bless you.

FRESH START TODAY

A promise from our Savior, Jesus Christ by Lenni Nordloh

Titus 3:4-7, But when the kindness and love of God our Savior appeared, he saved us, not because of righteous things

> *we had done, but because of his mercy. He saved us through the washing of rebirth and renewal by the Holy Spirit, whom he poured out on us generously through Jesus Christ our Savior, so that, having been justified by his grace, we might become heirs having the hope of eternal life. NIV*

The Book of Romans clearly walks you through God's plan of Salvation. You can use it to instruct others to understand God's plan. (Romans 10:9) There may be people reading this devotional who do not know God's plan for their lives. I would be in error if I only wrote for believers because the Lord loves all sinners. The Lord never intended for people to die in their sin and face eternal separation from God. This statement seems harsh, but I needed to hear it, too. God speaks about the heart all the way through the Bible, and this is how the Holy Spirit touches humanity with His love. We must love the sinner and not judge too harshly the people who have not received this wonderful promise. I used to say "by the grace of God there go I!" There are many believers who can say that before accepting Christ as their Savior they used to be worldly, gossiping, backbiting and unkind. That is sin, my friend. We are not right before God because of our own actions and attitudes. Righteousness is a church word that just means we can be right before God due to the death and resurrection of Jesus Christ. He is the Holy veil that hides our sins and intercedes for us on a daily basis as we pray to the Holy Father. He sifts the words of our prayers, and God the Father hears our heart's attitude.

I have a friend and sister in Christ who was brought by a co-worker of hers to a Bible study class that I used to teach. The class was for women who had circumstances in their lives where they could freely speak and not be judged. What was talked about in the class stayed in the classroom. This woman used to attend the class sitting with her arms closed across her chest and a frown on her face. She listened to the women as they shared their concerns. She would not come for 2 or 3 weeks and then would show up again. This occurred over several months. We honestly cared about her and began to pray for her to see the love of Jesus Christ. The Holy Spirit started to work in her heart as she began to forgive issues that she could not release without His help. Her heart began to change, and in God's time she said to the ladies, "I thought you were all phonies because of the love that was shared in the classroom, but now I know that it is real!" The tears began to flow as we all recognized the activity of the Holy Spirit. This is why we are not to judge others because only God knows the issues of a heart. He knows how to reach the individual, but we need to be available to share the truth about God's love. The Lord gives mercy and grace to those that would pray to accept this promised gift.

A wise preacher once said that the Good News (Gospel) of Christ is either substantiated or negated by the love and unity the church demonstrates. The reason some people do not understand how to accept the love of Jesus Christ is because they have been battered by others they thought they could trust. Your continued love for the unlovely is what may lighten the burden of their pain. The Holy Spirit will give you the strength to say and do what you need to do for this person.

Read the scripture for today and listen for truth that is being said. May the Lord bless you this new day as you begin fresh in your relationship with the Lord.

FRESH START TODAY

God, May your will be done! by Lenni Nordloh

> *Matthew 26:36-42, Then Jesus came with them to a place called Gethsemane, and said to the disciples, "Sit here while I go and pray over there." And He took with Him Peter and the two sons of Zebedee, and He began to be sorrowful and deeply distressed. Then He said to them, "My soul is exceedingly sorrowful, even to death. Stay here and watch with Me." He went a little farther and fell on His face, and prayed, saying, "O My Father, if it is possible, let this cup pass from Me; nevertheless, not as I will, but as You will." Then He came to the disciples and found them sleeping, and said to Peter, "What! Could you not watch with Me one hour? Watch and pray, lest you enter into temptation. The spirit indeed is willing, but the flesh is weak." Again, a second time, He went away and prayed, saying, "O My Father, if*

> *this cup cannot pass away from Me unless I drink it, Your will be done." NKJV*

What is the message that Jesus shared with the world that is so very important? Jesus was troubled and He knew that prayer was needed at this time. He wanted to be close to the Father, and He knew what was about to happen to Him. Was He afraid? He was sorrowful and troubled, but I do not believe He was afraid. His sorrow was deep to the point of death. He was human, but fully God. He cried out "God, not my will, but your will be done!" This cry was for men, women and children! He loves us! Jesus began the first steps towards giving humanity His grace and redemption. He would be crossing the barrier caused by human sin to bridge the gap between God and man. He would become the sin sacrifice once for all sin! Do you suppose the Father may have given Jesus the peace and strength that He needed to follow through with doing the will of God through time He spent in prayer? Why was Jesus silent and willing to allow humanity to torture Him? The strength of the powerful God enabled our Lord to endure more than any human being could endure and still live. He gave up His life willingly. Man did not kill Him! Man's sin killed Him!

Jesus asked an important question of Peter when He asked "could you not keep watch with me for one hour?" Could we watch and pray to God for one hour today? There is a spiritual benefit to praying this way, and it is to keep us from falling into temptation. We gain the peace and strength that Jesus received. We begin to grasp and understand the will of God!

There may have been a time that you were too frightened to surrender to God's will and not your own. You will never be asked to sacrifice your life for the sins of the world. The one pure Lamb of God has already done that. You may be asked to leave your family to serve where God is working. You may be asked to teach a Bible Study Class when you have never done it before or never wanted to do something like this due to your shyness. You may not speak clearly, but the Holy Spirit through you can and will.

Have you said things backwards in a conversation? Well, a confession is in order from my heart to yours, just recently, when I began to pray I started by saying "God, not your will, but mine"! God knew what my heart was really feeling, so He allowed me to say it out loud! The shock of what I said surprised me! This has stayed with me for several days, and I keep asking myself "Am I truly wanting God's will or my own?" Jesus said the "The Spirit is willing, but the flesh is weak!" Do we really trust the heart of God? Do we understand that He desires the best for us, or do we think He just wants to punish us? Did Jesus really die for your sin? Jesus walked the path to the cross, so that we would see His love for us. Has He changed His mind? Can you say when you spend that hour in prayer that you see the love of Jesus penetrating your heart with His peace, strength and love? Maybe we can learn to pray "Not my will be done, but yours, God". Do not be afraid, because a blessing is waiting to be revealed to you.

FRESH START TODAY

Wisdom that comes from God – by Lenni Nordloh

> *Proverbs 2:6-11, For the Lord gives wisdom; From His mouth come knowledge and understanding; He stores up sound wisdom for the upright; He is a shield to those who walk uprightly; He guards the paths of justice, And preserves the way of His saints. Then you will understand righteousness and justice, Equity and every good path. When wisdom enters your hear, And knowledge is pleasant to your soul, Discretion will preserve you; Understanding will keep you, NKJV*

Proverbs is the book that was written by King Solomon who desired and asked for wisdom above anything else in prayer to God. He wanted the wisdom to rule God's people justly and rightly. God gave him what he asked for and more. Was Solomon so different than the rest of humanity? Do we have the ability to ask God for the same wisdom? What a wonderful and beautiful gift. We could ask God for the wisdom to understand His grace that has been given to believers through Jesus Christ our Lord. He would open the doors to understanding because this would please the Lord. People are so caught up with their daily lives that they do not stop to ask for wisdom for the day. A fresh start of wisdom for every day would be a blessing! We have decisions to make and actions to take, so why not include the Lord in our daily activity? What a blessing to acknowledge and surrender to the Holy Spirit to assist us in our every move during the day. To know that we have invited the Lord to be with us could make us direct our thoughts and actions in a different light. Could it not?

We sometimes desire to help change others, but do you suppose the Lord may want us to be silent and allow the Holy Spirit to change others that need changing? A spiritual sister once said that if we all prayed for blessings of wisdom on our enemies as well as those that we love we would witness the activity of the Holy Spirit. When we do this it seems the burden drops off our shoulders and drop on to Jesus, giving Him the rains to choose the blessings. Do you suppose that He has more experience in changing a heart than we might know? God is a big boy and He can handle humanity much better than we do. He may choose to work through us, but we must have a humble heart of love for the Holy Spirit to be able to touch another heart. It may be like watching a clear river flow down a mountain ravine that does not have branches or large rocks to stop the flow. We can become stiff necked (the large branches) and judgmental (the large rocks). We bow or bend like a large branch in the water. This hinders the direct flow, and the river has to go around us in order to get where it needs to travel. The branch may actually cause muddy waters if it stays stiff necked. The flow of the Holy Spirit is amazing to watch when God is working in the heart of a person. It takes time to build the character of Jesus Christ in the heart of any person due to our humanity and sinful nature.

There may be times when we have to let go and let God do what He wants to do through our lives. God hates the proud but lifts up those who are humble. (I Peter 5:6) He is blessed when we have total faith in His wisdom. He knows what is best. The scriptures tell us today that when we ask for wisdom, we will know what is just, fair and right, and it will be pleasant to our souls. God's discernment through the power of the Holy Spirit will protect us and guard our hearts.

Sometimes our prayers need to be "Lord help change me!"

FRESH START TODAY

Learn to Fly Like an Eagle! - By Lenni Nordloh

> *Isaiah 40:3, But those who wait on the Lord Shall renew their strength; They shall mount up with wings like eagles, They shall run and not be weary, They shall walk and not faint. NKJV*

This morning as I praised the Father in Heaven I began to remember the Old Testament stories of how God communicated, provided and desired a relationship with His people. He spoke to Moses, Gideon, Jeremiah, King David, Samuel and the list goes on and on. In the book of Hebrews names are mentioned to honor the people of faith. As I prayed, I began to thank the Lord for His written Word. When we search the scriptures, we can find the very nature and personality of the God of the Universe. He related to mankind in a personal way through centuries, as people were inspired to write the stories of their relationship with the living God. King David poured his heart out to God through the music of the Psalms, and we learn about a God that loves the music that comes from a dedicated and faithful heart.

The scripture that I am relating to today are the words that my son used to put all over His wall when he was a teenager. People gave him gifts of eagles. I truly believe that my son hung on to these scriptures for many years as he suffered through many disappointments in his life, but there is a deeper meaning I have now come to understand.

Just recently I have been studying lessons by Kay Arthur on *Teach Me to Pray*, and she encourages believers to fly spiritually! She said that by reading God's Word daily and praying is like the power of the wings of a bird. You cannot fly without both wings being in motion. A Fresh start today gives us the opportunity to soar like eagles as we seek the face of the living God through reading the Word and praying.

I mentioned in a previous devotion that God did not give me breast cancer, but He allowed it only to draw me closer to Him. Through the trials of treatments I did become weary at times, but the presence of the Holy Spirit abounded through my husband, friends and family in their prayers and encouragement. I have renewed my strength and feel better physically than I have in several years. I owe my dedication and my praise to God the Father, God the Son and God the Holy Spirit for blessing me with healing. I am honored to bring Glory to God, and He deserves the best that I can offer Him in being available to bring others to the truth of what Jesus Christ has done for mankind. When we experience the trials that God allows us to experience, we can grow to know the heart of God.

Reading the experiences of those who have gone before us we realize that human nature doubts from time to time. Jonah (who ran from God) and Job (who lost his family and all his earthly riches) are examples of trial and many doubts. The Lord blessed those he loved at the end of their trials, and they grew to know the nature of our God. Job was humbled to the majestic God who revealed His wisdom and power to him at the end. Sin is forgiven, but there may be consequences of sin we must endure for us to become more like Jesus Christ.

Our hope must be in the Lord to receive the promise of renewed strength. We take flight like the wings of the eagle as we take time to grow in faith through reading God's Word and talking to the Lord daily. I have learned that doing things for the Lord is not what He desires, but growing to know Him and His love is what blesses Him the most. I remember that God wanted to provide, give land flowing with milk and honey and have a relationship with His people when they fled slavery in Egypt. He has not changed His desire for His people today. We need to trust His heart and have a desire to know Him.

Jesus Christ has given the believer GRACE that we cannot earn, but is a gift from God the Father. He has provided the sinner a way to become pure before a Holy God.

FRESH START TODAY

God is fulfilling His Promise – by Lenni Nordloh

> *Romans 4:13-25, "It was not through law that Abraham and his offspring received the promise that he would be heir of the world, but through the righteousness that comes by faith.*

*For if those who live by law are heirs, faith has no value and the promise is worthless, because law brings wrath. And where there is no law there is no transgression. Therefore, **the promise comes by faith**, so that it may be by grace and may be guaranteed to all Abraham's offspring — not only to those who are of the law but also to those who are of the faith of Abraham. He is the father of us all. As it is written: '**I have made you a father of many nations**.' He is our father in the sight of God, in whom he believed — the God who gives life to the dead and calls things that are not as though they were. Against all hope, Abraham in hope believed and so became the father of many nations, just as it had been said to him, "So shall your offspring be." Without weakening in his faith, he faced the fact that his body was as good as dead — since he was about a hundred years old — and that Sarah's womb was also dead. Yet he did not waver through unbelief regarding the promise of God, but was strengthened in his faith and gave glory to God, being fully persuaded that God had power to do what he had promised. This is why 'it was credited to him as righteousness.' The words 'it was credited to him' were written not for him alone, but also for us, to whom God will credit righteousness — for us who believe in him who raised Jesus our Lord from the dead. He was delivered over to death for our sins and was raised to life for our justification." NIV*

WHAT WOULD YOUR HEART TELL YOU TO DO IF YOU KNEW, WITHOUT A DOUBT, THAT YOU WERE A DIRECT DECENDANT OF KING DAVID OF ISREAL?

My brother called me up several days in a row asking me to continue researching our family history. I had lost interest for several years because the information was not easily available unless a lot of money was spent to get on to certain web sites. My husband and I agreed that we would sign up for two months to research in the Ancestry.com web site. My father's

171

side of the family had stopped with Thomas Roberts from Ireland about 1790 and then there was a dead-end.

My mother's side began to open up to my surprise. What is amazing is that she was an only child and orphaned by the time she was 17 years old. Mother never talked about her family due to the heartache she experienced growing up. She often felt very alone. She would never know, in her lifetime, how special she really was and how her life would bless the rest of our family of God. The research began in a book of history on the life of Henry Sater from Baltimore. This man was my 6th great grandfather. His wife's mother (My 7th great-grandmother) was the great-granddaughter to Sir Oliver Cromwell, Lord Protector of England. This information was somehow over looked in the previous research, so from Sir Oliver Cromwell, the family history exploded! Spending many hours for several days looking up 46 lines of Royalty, beginning with Queen Catherine (1431 – 1495) and Sir Owen Meredith Tudor to Julia Victoria Ferch Prasutagus Princess of Icenti (45-91). The research was exciting, but one day I started praying, asking God, what good was this historical information?

My research stopped for a few days and then the Holy Spirit prompted me to continue. The next generation back from where the research had stopped was "Prasutagus "Druid king of Britian, Icenti" Icenians (-61) was the son of Anna "The Prophetess who was the daughter of Joseph of Arimathea. This information humbled me with praise on my lips to a Holy God that wanted me to understand a deeper truth about His plan. I have all the documentation that went back to David, king of Israel, which has revealed that he was my 101st great-grandfather. I decided not to include all of this history information. Reading all those names would be like reading a telephone book. The Bible has documented genealogies and most people scan over all those Hebrew names. The importance of this research was NOT my family line, but God's plan working through people through many generations. He has promised that a thousand generations would be blessed for those who have trusted the Lord and followed His commandments.

It is just "Simply a Whisper" – Learn to listen for the still small voice of God – He will bless you! God promised Abraham that he would be a father of many nations. Are you, as a believer, ready to listen? The promise comes by faith. God has always had a plan. It is not how big we are, as believers, but how big do you think God is?

Paul stated, in the scriptures that if he had reasons to put confidence in the flesh, he did. (Philippians 4-6). I agree with Paul, still knowing that God has a plan, the flesh is not to be worshiped.

> *Phillippians 7-9, But whatever was my profit I now consider loss for the sake of Christ. What is more, I consider everything a loss compared to the surpassing greatness of knowing Christ Jesus my Lord, for whose sake I have lost all things. I consider them rubbish, that I may gain Christ, and be found in Him, not having a righteousness of my own that comes from the law, but that through faith in Christ – the righteousness that comes from God and is by faith. NIV*

Glory to God, the creator of heaven and earth! Did God truly reveal Himself through ordinary people in the Bible? Will He continue to reveal Himself to people today?

1.   *Pray:*
Lord, I see that every person that belongs to you by faith has a story. I can see that your promise to Abraham is being fulfilled and I know that I am part of your plan. Jesus is the King of Kings and I praise your name! I see you have always had a plan for my life and that is to do your will. The most important truth is that when I accepted Jesus Christ as my Savior and my name has been written in the Lamb's Book of Life. I have a spiritual heritage with you, Lord.

2.   *Reflection:*
What have you learned about God's plan? Did you see a line of believers that did God's will? Did you see sinners? Is God's promise to Abraham being fulfilled? Do you understand how special you are to God?

CONCLUSION

How do you conclude a book on simply a whisper? We have learned that the power of the Holy Spirit indwells every believer and that He will whisper to the spiritually sensitive heart. The message reveals that there is freedom through Jesus Christ. We have witnessed God's blessings through the whisper in nature, in God's plan, in the Word, through Grace, through Mercy, through music, through generations past, through forgiveness, through victorious testimonies, through angels, through prayer, when witnessing, through the heart of another believer, through the seasons of life and finally reach freedom. Every man, woman and child is created uniquely, so that God can work through the human heart in different ways. He desires to have a personal relationship with all people who would trust His heart. He wants you to know that He is still present and desires to be glorified through your life. God desires to lift those up who humble their hearts to a loving God. I am thankful that God has allowed me to take you with me on a spiritual journey. The reading of the Word continues to bless a believer as God reveals more about the Father, Jesus and the Holy Spirit through the Scriptures. God is the creator of heaven and earth. He controls and keeps the weather in balance, the universe in balance, and observes the human heart. He created the land and the ocean boundaries so that man can live comfortably.

God has been disappointed in the rebellion and sin that runs rampant in our world. He has promised that judgment will come sometime in the future. You need to be concerned if you are not a believer, but there is still time for you to turn from your sin. There is still time to accept Jesus Christ as your Lord and Savior. There is still time to desire to know the God who has provided a plan for you and your loved ones. There is still time to adjust your life to how God wants to communicate with you.

You may have a family who has shown you the path to Jesus Christ. You may have struggled with a family who did not know the Lord. God will guide you to a better future and your descendants as you grow to understand His love. You can be the faithful one who will encourage those that follow you to trust, by faith, in the Lord Jesus Christ.

Prayer is a way that the Holy Spirit will whisper to you that will change your heart. The joy and peace that a person receives when he or she spends time in prayer is amazing. You get acquainted with God and His character. He is absolutely fabulous!

When you listen to God's music, you are drawn to a musical God who wants to soften and encourage you to worship Him. Music can prompt you to praise and pray to Jesus. An Evangelist Preacher once said that all preachers would lose their jobs when they get to heaven. The musicians would take over by singing praises in God's choir for all eternity. You can use music to open or close your prayer time with the Lord.

May the Lord bless you as you walk the path to Calvary's cross with Jesus, where He chose to die for you. Grace is a wonderful gift to humanity. Mercy is something that is offered to us so that we do not receive what you and I really deserve. The dark path that you walked brought you to understand that forgiveness brings you freedom.

You learned that God answers prayers that could brighten your future when you read the story of a runaway teenager who became a preacher's wife. You read about the peace that God gave a believer who lost her husband in the 1995 Oklahoma federal building bombing. God listens to your prayers. He whispers to you to give you understanding. He desires to be close to His people.

Jesus gave us an example of how we should treat each other. He commanded us to love one another, and this will show the world that we are His disciples. He warned us about the roaring lion that is out to devour anyone who is weak. Jesus won the battle over the serpent, so we should trust in the power that has our heart. Those who believe receive more than we deserve because Jesus is on our side. President Ronald Reagan once said, in a speech, "The real question is, are we really on God's side?"

John 15:9-17, "As the Father loved Me, I also have loved you; abide in My love. If you keep My commandments, you will abide in My love, just as I have kept My Father's commandments and abide in His love. "These things I have spoken to you, that My joy may remain in you, and that your joy may be full. This is My commandment, that you love one another as I have loved you. Greater love has no one than this, than to lay down one's life for his friends. You are My friends if you do whatever I command you. No longer do I call you servants, for a servant does not know what his master is doing; but I have called you friends, for all things that I heard from My Father I have made known to you. You did not choose Me, but I chose you and appointed you that you should go and bear fruit, and that your fruit should remain, that whatever you ask the Father in My name He may give you. These things I command you, that you love one another.
NKJV

SIMPLY A WHISPER

Simply a whisper from you, Dear Father
Is all I long to hear
To Guide My Heart and Keep My Path Sure
From Envy, and Strife and Fear

Teach Me to Hear Your Still small voice
Above All the noise of the World
And know without Doubt that you're Talking to me
As your plan for my life is unfurled

Help Me to bend my ear Ever close
To your heart so that we may be one
That I may be worthy of Heaven with you
Forever to Worship Your Son

Written by Charlotte Slaving,
Nash, Oklahoma
(Written with verbal consent specifically for this book)